CW00944057

Caravan

Teacher's Book

1

Liz Hocking

MACMILLAN

Macmillan Education
Between Towns Road, Oxford OX4 3PP
A division of Macmillan Publishers Limited
Companies and representatives throughout the world

ISBN 1 4050 0251 4

Text © Liz Hocking 2004
Design and illustrations © Macmillan Publishers Ltd 2004

First published 2004

All rights reserved; no part of this publication may be reproduced, stored in a
retrieval system, transmitted in any form, or by any means, electronic, mechanical,
photocopying, recording, or otherwise, without the prior written permission of the
publishers.

Design and layout by Anne Sherlock Design
Illustrated by Juliet Breese
Cover design by Linda Reed and Associates

Printed and bound in Egypt by Zamzam Presses

2008 2007 2006 2005 2004
10 9 8 7 6 5 4 3 2 1

Contents

Scope and Sequence

Topic	Structures	Vocabulary	Phonics
Welcome page 10	Informal greetings. Classroom language for teacher use: *Point to … . Give me … . Bring me … . Open … . Close … . Show me … . Stand up. Sit down. Find … . Come here. Go to your desk.*	*father, mother, brother, sister*	Alphabet
1 My friends page 18	Lessons 1–6 *Hello. I'm …* Lessons 7–10, 12 *What is it? It's a … What number is it? Find …* Lesson 11 Review	*pen, pencil, book, bag, crayon, pencil case, rubber, ruler* 1, 2, 3, 4, 5, 6, 7, 8, 9, 10	Initial letter sounds: *a–i*
2 My class page 42	Lessons 1–4 *What's your name? How old are you? I'm … Bring me …* Lessons 5–10, 12 *It's (black).* Lesson 11 Review	*scissors, chalk, paper, box please green, yellow, blue, red, black, white*	Initial letter sounds: *j–r*
3 My colours page 66	Lessons 1–6 *It's a (yellow plane). What colour is the …/it? It's (blue and white).* Lessons 7–10, 12 *How many … ?* Plural *s* Lesson 11 Review	*bird, plane, tree, balloon dry, wash, wipe, clean orange, brown, pink, grey, purple thank you*	Initial letter sounds: *s–z*
4 My favourite things page 90	Lessons 1–6 *Is it a … ? Yes./No. I need a … . Give me a … .* Lessons 7–10, 12 *a/an Is it big/small? Yes./No, it's … .* Lesson 11 Review	*bat, teddy, doll, kite, plate, spoon, cup, glass big, small train, car, boat, bike*	Initial letter recognition: *c* and *h, h* and *p*
5 My animal pictures page 114	Lessons 1–6 *What can you see? I can see a /an … . It begins with … .* Lessons 7–10, 12 *Can you see … ? Yes./No. I can see … .* Lesson 11 Review	*horse, donkey, camel, snake tie, feed, be careful of fish, mouse, frog, bee*	Initial letter recognition: *t* and *b, p* and *c*
6 My fun games page 138	Lessons 1–6 *I can … / I can't …* Lessons 7–10, 12 *True/False Can you … ? Yes./No.* Lesson 11 Review	*run, hop, jump, skip stop, wait, go, look right, left bus whistle, ride a bike, swim, count to ten*	Initial letter sounds: *r* and *m; v, b, p* and *s*

Reading	Writing	Speaking	Listening
Alphabet	Pre-writing tasks.	Informal greetings Alphabet Family Numbers 1–10	Informal greetings Alphabet Family Numbers 1–10
Alphabet Letters *Aa–Ii*	Letters *aA–gG* Numbers 1–6	Identifying people, objects and numbers. Acting a story. Singing a song.	Letter sounds *a–i* Alphabet exemplars
Letters *Jj–Rr*	Letters *hH–pP* Numbers 7–10	Asking about people. Identifying objects and colours. Talking about items. Acting a story. Singing a song.	Letter sounds *j–r* Alphabet exemplars
Letters *Ss–Zz*	Letters *qQ–zZ*	Describing items. Asking about colours. Talking about numbers. Acting a story. Singing a song.	Letter sounds *s–z* Alphabet exemplars
Ball, bat, kite, train, car, boat, bike	Tracing letters and whole words. Writing *a* and *an*.	Talking about colours and numbers. Describing items. Acting a story. Singing a song.	Initial letter recognition: *c* and *h*, *h* and *p*
cat, donkey, snake, camel, dog, horse, blue, green, yellow, fish, mouse, bee, frog, red, black, white	Tracing whole words. Writing *a* and *an*. Tracing capital letters and whole words. Writing whole words. Sentence completion.	Asking and answering questions about items. Giving instructions. Acting a story. Saying a rhyme.	Initial letter recognition: *t* and *b*, *p* and *c*
I can, I can't, run, hop, skip, jump, It's a, pink, purple, orange, count to 10, ride a bike, whistle, swim, yes, no, can you, brown, grey	Tracing and writing whole words. Sentence completion. Writing complete sentences.	Talking about actions. Acting a story. Singing a song.	Initial letter sounds: *r* and *m*; *v, b, p* and *s*

Introduction

Components of the course

The Pupil's Book

The Pupil's Book consists of six Topics chosen to appeal to Primary 1 children. Each topic is made up of twelve lessons covering a wide variety of activities aimed at developing all the skills children need to progress in their learning. There is also a five-page Welcome topic at the start to ensure that all students have the same basic level of understanding at the beginning of the course.

The Workbook

Each Pupil's Book lesson is accompanied by a page of Workbook exercises – except Lessons 6 and 11 in Topics 1 to 3, which have two pages of Workbook exercises. These practise language taught in the Pupil's Book. They develop, in particular, skills in reading and writing. Beginning with simple pencil control exercises, children progress through correct letter formation to tracing, copying and then writing words and phrases into grids. Most Workbook exercises in Topics 4 to 6 also require children to read what they have traced or copied.

The Tape

All new vocabulary and language structures are presented on recordings, giving children practice in listening and pronunciation. New language is often presented through dialogues featuring the course characters, so that right from the start children get used to hearing a variety of voices in a conversational context. Songs and rhymes reinforce the language being taught and give children the satisfaction of learning a complete piece of work in English.

Flashcards

There is a complete set of Flashcards to accompany the course. There are specific Flashcards for presenting the alphabet, with the small and capital letters on one side and the exemplar picture on the other. There are also Flashcards for presenting the main vocabulary as it is introduced in each topic, including the course characters, objects, actions, numbers and colours. As well as presenting vocabulary, the Flashcards can be used in a range of games.

The Teacher's Book

This contains a Scope and Sequence, detailed teaching notes for every lesson in the Pupil's Book and Workbook, a list of extra games, and a set of photocopiable resource pages. The latter can be used to produce picture cards for use in lessons.

Features of *Caravan 1*

Children learn in different ways and at different speeds. For this reason each lesson in this course provides a variety of activities and approaches to learning and practising English. The skills of reading, writing, listening and speaking are all developed systematically. They are covered through both formal exercises and active participation in songs, rhymes, acting out and games.

Welcome Topic

The Pupil's Book begins with a five-page Welcome topic. This covers the alphabet (small and capital letters) with exemplar vocabulary, numbers, colours and family members. The activities in this topic can be used to remind children of any English they have learned previously, and to help teachers to find out how much children already know and can remember. The material need not be learned and drilled exhaustively as it is covered systematically in Topics 1 to 3. Children then move on to new work in Topic 4 with a firm grounding in the key language.

The Welcome topic also presents classroom instructions that the class can learn so that lessons can be largely conducted in English. Teaching methods in Topics 1 to 6 encourage the use of this language. However, explanations and discussions that will help children to understand the content of the lesson should be done in their first language.

Games

Games are an important feature of *Caravan 1* and they are designed to involve and motivate children whilst practising and recycling what they have learned. At first the games can be led by the teacher, with children responding. As teacher and class become more skilled in games, there is greater opportunity for the teacher to demonstrate the activity which the children then work on alone or in groups. Many of the games are illustrated in the Pupil's Book and are suitable for whole-class and pair work. Additional games are suggested in the teaching notes for most lessons. A list of these games is on page 9. This can be used for quick reference when a few extra minutes are available at the end of a lesson, or to find a game you may wish to repeat.

Resources

In addition to the components of the course, teachers may wish to make use of the photocopiable material on pages 162–168 at the end of this book. Resources are provided for creating sets of small cards for use in games and activities throughout *Caravan 1*. These include alphabet exemplar pictures, letters, numbers, words and phrases. As well as being useful for the whole class, these cards can be particularly helpful for small-group work and for consolidating the learning of slower children.

Teacher's Book Lesson Notes

Every topic in this book begins with a summary of all the skills and activities that are covered in the twelve lessons. Each lesson begins with a lesson profile, which includes:

Pupil's Book and Workbook pages: representations of the material the children will use in each lesson in the form of facsimile pages

Performance indicators: a list of the skills that children will be able to demonstrate by the end of the lesson

New language: the structures and vocabulary to be introduced in the lesson

Reading words: words which students will be taught to read in the lesson

Review language: the structures and vocabulary to be reviewed from previous lessons

Bring to the lesson: a list of the materials and teaching resources needed during the lesson

Preparation: instructions about the materials and teaching resources that need to be made or collected before the lesson begins (not every lesson requires preparation).

The notes for each lesson are always in the same format and include these components:

Warm-ups

Every lesson begins with a short session of activities which aim to achieve one or more of the following:

- further practice of the language from the previous lesson
- recycling of language learned in the previous few lessons
- revision of previously learned language for a task later in the lesson.

The Warm-ups are also a chance for teachers to check on progress of the whole class and of individuals. They practise listening and speaking in particular, and often give children a chance to co-operate with one another. Some Warm-up notes offer more than one activity: one or more can be chosen.

Presentation

Suggestions for preparing children for the first activity in their Pupil's Books are given after every Warm-up. The purpose of this is to focus children on the language they are going to use. Children are then able to respond to the Pupil's Book activities more readily, and need less explanation to do the task.

Pupil's Book Activities

There are usually two activities on each page and often the first of these leads into the second. The teaching notes suggest how to take the class through the activities so that children are actively involved in learning. In particular there are suggestions for pre-listening tasks before all recorded material, so that children are able to get the most benefit from hearing the language.

Extension Activities

Most lessons contain suggestions for one or more extra activities following on from those in the Pupil's Book. Some of these are for the whole class. Others can be done in pairs or groups. The resources pages at the end of the book include pictures that can be copied for use in Extension activities. Children who finish work ahead of the others can do this extra practice. These activities are always optional and children will not miss the core elements of each lesson if they are omitted.

Workbook Activities

These exercises require little teacher explanation but give plenty of practice in writing skills, vocabulary practice and simple reading tasks. Some exercises could be set or finished for homework.

Methodology

Reading

Topics 1 to 3 concentrate on the recognition of letters (capital and small), recognition of initial sounds, and on general skills that are needed before children begin to read. These include noticing differences and similarities between shapes and objects, predicting, and talking extensively about a picture, both finding details and interpreting the action. Words are presented alongside the alphabet exemplars in the first three units, but it is not intended that these should be learned and drilled by the whole class at this stage. Able children may be ready to read single words before others, and it may be appropriate to give these children word recognition activities in the early units, e.g. word and picture matching (see page 162, Resources pages). Words are introduced for reading by the whole class in Topics 4 to 6. Vocabulary items are presented for sight recognition. CVC (consonant-vowel-consonant) words are included for phonic recognition.

Writing

The Welcome topic contains pencil control exercises and reinforces left-to-right movement. It also gives teachers the opportunity to check pupils are holding their pencils correctly, and that they have a good writing position, before they move onto more formal writing exercises. Make sure that children have enough space to write comfortably, that they are seated at the correct height, and have their paper or book turned at a slight angle away from them.

A good writing position.

Right-handed writers should use their left hands to keep the paper or book in the correct position as they write, and vice versa for left-handed writers.

Workbook Topics 1 to 3 give extensive practice in letter formation and fluent letter writing. If children have had limited writing practice before, it may be appropriate to complete the controlled letter-writing practice for several letters, before children form the letters independently on the final grid.

Listening

Exercises to develop this skill include listening for instruction and for information. Other exercises help children to match sounds to language. There are recorded dialogues to accompany the picture story in every topic. These are designed to help children gain a feel for conversational language. For that reason many of them are suitable for acting out. The songs and rhymes in *Caravan 1* are all particularly well suited for memorising and reciting. This enables children to take in more complex passages of English and enjoy a sense of achievement.

Speaking

Every lesson gives extensive opportunites for children to speak individually, in groups and as a class. Speaking is modelled by the teacher, or on the recording, so that children can approach each task with confidence. Practice is essential for consolidating skills, and opportunities for children to speak in pairs are frequently given in the teaching notes. When you begin pair work, tell children they must speak very quietly. Keep the activity short and simple at the beginning until the class has become used to the activity. Always go around the class and listen to pairs as they work. The story dialogues, which children can act out, give conversational practice in a controlled context.

Games

All these games are suggested in the *Caravan 1* teaching notes. The lesson where they are first introduced is given in brackets. A more detailed explanation is given in the notes for that lesson. This list can be used to find games to repeat another time. Many of them can be adapted for different abilities, for pair work and small groups.

1 Instruction game (Welcome, page 11)
Class or individuals carry out your instructions, e.g. *Children, point to Omar. Maged, bring me your rubber*, etc.

2 Alphabet matching game (Welcome, page 13)
Children match alphabet exemplar pictures with matching letters.

3 Letter matching game (Welcome, page 13)
Children match capital and small letters.

4 Name the object game (Topic 1, Lesson 4)
Children have three or four small picture cards. Name an object. The children who have that picture hold up it up and repeat the word. Whole class repeats.

5 Flashcard numbers and pictures game (Topic 1, Lesson 6)
Put numbers beside Flashcards. One child says a number. Another child names the object in the picture.

6 Find number … . What is it? game (Topic 1, Lesson 11)
Write numbers beside Flashcards. Show Team A a number Flashcard. Team A says to Team B, e.g. *Find number 4. What is it?* Team B names the object beside the number given: *It's a … .*

7 Bring me the … , please game (Topic 2, Lesson 3)
Children bring real objects or Flashcards from around the room according to your instructions, e.g. *Dina, bring me the apple, please.*

8 Colour game (Topic 2, Lesson 5)
Children have small colour cards. Say a colour. All those with that colour stand up

9 Flashcard colour game (Topic 2, Lesson 6)
Class in teams. Team leaders hold a colour Flashcard. Name a colour. Team with that colour stand up together and say it. Change over team colours several times during the game.

10 Please instruction game (Topic 2, Lesson 9)
Give instructions, e.g. *Stand up, sit down, open your book*, etc. If the instruction ends with please, children do it. If not, they keep still. Any who move are out.

11 Stop and go game (Topic 3, Lesson 1)
Divide the class into numbered (or coloured) teams. Say, e.g., *2 (Red), go … . 4 (Yellow), go … . 2 (Red), stop … .1 (Blue), go*, etc. Children stand still for Stop and walk on the spot for Go. Change over the team numbers (colours), so children have to listen out for a different number (colour).

12 Number order action game (Topic 3, Lesson 5)
Children hold number Flashcards in mixed order. Class says numbers in order. Children with Flashcards get in order before the class counts to the last number.

13 Is it a … ? Yes/No, game (Topic 4, Lesson 2)
Put picture Flashcards on the board. Number them. Say *Number 3. Is it a ball?* Children answer *Yes, it's a ball./ No, it's a key.*

14 I need a … Memory chain game (Topic 4, Lesson 3)
First player says, e.g. *I need a pencil.* Second player repeats and adds another object, e.g. *I need a pencil and a rubber.* The third player continues, e.g. *I need a pencil, a rubber and a ruler.* Players keep adding on objects until somebody can't remember an item. Start again with different objects.

15 I can see a … Memory chain game (Topic 5, Lesson 2)
As game 14 but with *I can see* + animal. Example: *I can see a horse … I can see a horse and a camel … I can see a horse, a camel and a donkey.*

16 I can see a … Memory chain game (variation)
As game 15, but add colours, e.g. *I can see a green frog, a blue fish and a grey goat.*

Welcome

In this topic pupils:

- introduce themselves
- respond to a greeting
- understand and carry out eleven classroom instructions
- recognise and name the capital and small letters of the alphabet
- match capital and small letters
- name the exemplar vocabulary for each letter
- name family members
- name the numbers 1–10.

Section 1

Performance indicators

Children will be able to:
- introduce themselves
- respond to a greeting
- understand and carry out three classroom instructions.

New language

Hi, ...
I'm...

Bring to the lesson

- the Tape
- the Flashcard of Salama
- name cards for each child

Preparation

Make a name card for each child in the class.

 page 5   **page 1**

Warm-up

- Ask children what English words they can remember, e.g. the names of objects, colours and numbers. Make this very informal and praise children for what they can say. Correct errors simply by repeating correctly yourself without drilling.

- If children remember songs or chants in English ask them to sing or say them.

Presentation

- Give children a few moments to look through their

books. If you see that some children recognise or notice anything in particular, share the language with the class.

Listen and learn

- Children look at the picture of Salama. Hold up your book, point to him and say *Salama*. Children repeat.
- Tell children to listen. Play the Tape. Hold up your book. Point to Salama as he speaks.

Tapescript

Narrator: Welcome Unit. Section 1. Listen and learn.

Salama: Hi, children! I'm Salama.

- Play the Tape again or say the words yourself and point to Salama in your book. Hold up the Flashcard of Salama. Point and say *Salama*. Children repeat.
- Stick the Flashcard of Salama on the board. Wave and say *Hi, Salama*. Prompt children to do the same.
- Explain to children that Salama is a friend who is going to help them learn English.

Introducing oneself

- Wave and say to the class *Hi. I'm … (your name)*. Prompt the class to reply *Hi, Mr/Mrs/Miss …* .
- Bring three or four confident children to the front. They stand in a line facing the class. Prompt the first child to say, e.g. *Hi! I'm (Omar)*. Prompt the class to reply *Hi, (Omar)*. Continue with the other children in the line.
- Choose children around the class to stand up and introduce themselves. The class responds *Hi, …* .

Introducing the classroom instructions

- Hold up your book. Point to the first picture at the top on the right. Say *Point* and do the action a few times. Say *Point to Salama*. Prompt children to point to Salama.
- Indicate the second picture. Say *Give*. Say to a child, e.g. *Dina, give me your book*. Prompt the child to give you the book. Do not try to explain the whole sentence, but say *Give* clearly. Repeat with one or two other children.
- Ask for a few different objects, e.g. *a pencil*, etc. If the word is new, indicate the object you are asking for.

- Point to the third picture. Say *Bring*. Say to a child who is not near you, e.g. *Adam, bring me your book*. Give plenty of praise when the instruction is carried out.
- Do this again with other children. Ask for different objects they know the words for.

Extension activities

- Children take turns to come forward, hold up the Salama Flashcard and say to the class *Hi, children. I'm Salama*. Class replies *Hi, Salama*.
- Play the *Instruction game*. Say to the class or individuals, e.g. *Children, point to Omar. Maged, bring me your rubber. Natalia, give me your book*, etc. Praise children for carrying out the instruction correctly.

 page 1

Colour and say

- Children look at the picture. Say *Hi, children. I'm Salama*. Class repeats.
- Children colour the picture.

Draw, say and write

- Give each child their own name card. They draw themselves in the Workbook and copy their name into the blank. Go around helping.
- When children finish, they say the words in the bubble, adding their own name.

Section 2

Performance indicators

Children will be able to:
- recognise and name the capital and small letters of the alphabet
- match capital and small letters
- name the exemplar vocabulary for each letter
- understand and carry out five new classroom instructions.

New language

The alphabet
Exemplar vocabulary

Review language

Greetings and introductions

Bring to the lesson

- the Flashcard of Salama
- the alphabet Flashcards a–z
- small letter cards for a–z

Preparation

See page 162 for instructions on how to make the small letter cards a–z.

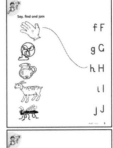

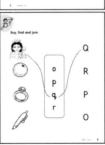

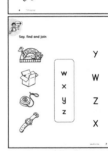

 PB **pages 6 and 7** WB **pages 2–7**

Warm-up

- Bring several children to the front. In turn they greet the class and introduce themselves, e.g. *Hi. I'm Sammy*. The class responds *Hi, Sammy*.

- Hold up the Flashcard of Salama and say his words from page 5 (*Hi, children. I'm Salama*). Class replies *Hi, Salama*. Let children come forward, show Salama and say his words. Class replies.

Presentation

Introducing the alphabet, a–e

- Show letters *A* and *a* on the first Flashcard and say the name of the letter. Children repeat. Write the letters *A* and *a* on the board. Point to the capital and say the name. Children repeat. Do the same with the small letter. Show the picture and say *apple*. Children repeat. Stick the Flashcard on the board above the letters with the picture facing the class.

- Continue in the same way with two more letters and exemplars, then revise all three, pointing in turn to the letters and pictures and eliciting the names.

- Introduce the fourth and fifth letters and exemplars, then revise all five.

 PB **pages 6 and 7**

My alphabet

- Let children look at both pages for a minute then focus attention on the top row. Tell them to listen and point. Say *a, apple*. Children repeat. Check they are pointing to the correct picture.

- Continue in the same way with the other four letters and pictures.

- Use the Flashcards and the letters written on the board. Drill the five letters and the exemplar vocabulary in alphabet order, then in any order.

Revising the colours

- Point out the borders round the letters, and Salama colouring the first box. Point to each box along the top row. Prompt the class to name the colours. (The last column on the right, with the grey outlines, is meant to represent white.)

- Children colour the borders for the letters they learn in each lesson. (For the last column, representing white, the children just leave the border plain.)

- Call out the colour of one of the borders in the row you have just taught. Children name the letter and exemplar in that colour box

Introducing the classroom instructions

- Hold up your book and point to the pictures at the bottom of page 7. Give children a moment to look at the different actions.

- Tell them to look at you. Demonstrate *Open*. Hold a book, say *Open* and open it. Say *Close* and close the book. Practise these instructions with the class and individuals.

- Say *Show me* and do as the picture in the book. Practise with individuals using the alphabet page, e.g. *Leila, show me the cat.*

- Introduce *Stand up* and *Sit down*. Use hand gestures to prompt the correct action. Practise all five instructions with the whole class and with individuals.

> **Note:** Once children are familiar with the classroom instructions, you may wish to introduce *Please* and *Thank you* to accompany some or all of them.

Extension activities

Play the *Alphabet matching game*.

- Put the alphabet Flashcards for a–e on the board, with the pictures facing the class. Put letter cards for a–e in any order underneath.

- Children take turns to come forward and put the correct letter beside the pictures.

- Point to each set of cards in turn. Children say *a, apple*, etc.

Play the *Letter matching game*.

- Write the capital letters in any order across the board. Put the small letter cards in any order below.

- Children come forward and put the small letter cards next to the correct capital letter.

> **Note:** These two games can be played with any number of exemplars and letters. Alphabet exemplars may be photocopied from pages 163–167. See page 162 for instructions on how to make the small letter cards a–z. These can be used to help children practise the matching activities individually, in pairs or small groups.

 page 2

Say and join

> **Note:** Before starting this exercise, see the suggestions for preparing the class for writing correctly and beginning to write on paper (Introduction, page 8).

- Using pencils, children draw over the lines joining the objects on the left with the letters on the right.

 pages 6 and 7

Presentation

Introducing the alphabet, f–z

- Teach the other letters and exemplars over the next few lessons, using Pupil's Book pages 6 and 7, the Flashcards and the small letter cards as before (see **Introducing the alphabet, a–e, My alphabet** and **Extension activities** above). It is recommended that you spend five lessons teaching the letters f–z (using the activity from the accompanying Workbook page at the end of each lesson) as follows: f–j (Workbook page 3); k–n (Workbook page 4); o–r (Workbook page 5); s–v (Workbook page 6); w–z (Workbook page 7).

- The letters and exemplars taught in each lesson should be revised in the following alphabet lessons so that children practise and gradually extend their vocabulary.

 pages 3–7

Say, find and join

- Children match exemplars to the correct small and capital letters.

Extension activity

Play the *Alphabet and colours game*.

- Divide the class into three teams. Team A names a letter, e.g. *d*. Team B says the colour of the box, *green*. Team C names the exemplar, *dog*. Teams take it in turns to name the letter.

Section 3

Performance indicators

Children will be able to:
- name family members
- understand and carry out three new classroom instructions.

New language

father, mother, brother, sister

Review language

Classroom instructions

Bring to the lesson

- the Tape
- the small letter cards for a–z from Section 2
- a set of alphabet exemplar picture cards

Preparation

Use Resources pages 163–167 to make a set of alphabet exemplar picture cards.

 PB **page 8**

Warm-up

- Play the *Alphabet game*, matching small letters to exemplars. Children play in groups of five or six. Each group should have five or six small letter cards and the matching exemplar picture cards. You may need two sets of each of the cards to do this.

Presentation

> **Note:** *Father* and *Mother* are used in formal conversations and situations. The informal terms *Mum* and *Dad* are often used in everyday conversation, especially by children.

- Teach the words for family members. Hold up your book and point to the picture of the father. Say *father*. Children repeat several times.

- Do the same for *mother*. Point to each in turn. The children say the words.

- Introduce *brother* and *sister* in the same way. Then point to the family members in any order. Children say the words.

PB **page 8**

Listen, point and say

- Children look at the pictures. Hold up your book. Point to the characters in any order. The class names them.

- Tell children to listen and be ready to point in their books. Play the first part of the Tape. Children point to the characters as they hear Salama introduce them.

Tapescript

Narrator: Welcome Unit. Section 3. Listen, point and say.

Salama: Meet my family. This is my father [pause], my mother [pause], my brother [pause] and my sister.

- Play the Tape again. Children repeat the family member in the pause.

- Play the second part of the Tape. Children find the characters in the pause and point to them as they speak.

- If you choose, you can pause the Tape after each character speaks for children to reply *Hello*. (This form of greeting is introduced in detail in Unit 1.)

Tapescript

Narrator: Now listen, find and say.

Salama: Hi, children. Meet my family. This is my mother. [pause]

Mother: Hello, children.

Salama: This is my sister. [pause]

Sister: Hello.

Salama: This is my father. [pause]

Father: Hello.

Salama: This is my brother. [pause]

Brother: Hello, everyone.

Introducing the classroom instructions

- Children look at the pictures at the bottom of the page for a moment or two. Hold up your book. Point to the first picture. Say *Find*. Demonstrate with some classroom objects in a bag. Go to a child and say, e.g. *Karim, find the pencil*. The child picks out the object.

- Repeat with other children, changing one or two of the objects each time.

- Point to the second picture and say *Come here*. Name a child. Say *Come here, (please)*. Keep the child by you.

- Point to the third picture and say *Go to your desk*, then say it to the child you called out. Repeat these last two instructions with several more children.

- Revise all the classroom instructions giving tasks to individuals and the whole class.

Section 4

Performance indicators

Children will be able to:
● name the numbers 1–10.

New language

The numbers 1–10

Review language

Family members
Classroom instructions

Bring to the lesson

● the Flashcards for the numbers 1–10
● one set of the alphabet exemplar picture cards from Section 3
● the small letter cards for a-z
● the Tape
● a list of classroom instructions

Preparation

Write a list of the different classroom instructions taught in the Welcome topic (see Extension activity). If you wish, list a task for each child, e.g. *Yussef, open your book,* etc.

 page 9

Warm-up

● Play *the Letters matching game* with capital letters written on the board and sets of small letter cards for children to stick beside them.

● Say *father, mother, brother, sister* as a chant, or revise the words using page 8 of the Pupil's Book.

Presentation

● Use the number Flashcards to revise the numbers 1–10. Hold up each Flashcard in order. The children say the number.

● Stick the Flashcards on the board. Point to them in order. Children say them.

● Point in any order, children say them.

 page 9

Listen and sing

● Children look at the numbers in their books. Tell them to listen and point to the numbers as they hear them. Play the Tape.

Tapescript

Narrator: Welcome Unit. Section 4. Listen and sing.

Song: 1, 2, 3, 4, 5,

6, 7, 8, 9, 10.

Now we can say our numbers,

Let's do it all again.

● Play the Tape again and encourage the children to join in with the numbers.

- Go through the last two lines with the class, a line at a time. Children repeat.
- Play the Tape a third time and encourage children to sing the whole song.

Play the game

Play the *Hands up/Stand up numbers game*.

- Divide the class into ten groups. Give each one a number Flashcard and tell them to hold it so you can see it.
- Say a number. Children in that group put their hands up or stand up. If they all do it together and quickly, give them a point.
- Call out each number at least once, then groups swap Flashcards. Call out the numbers more quickly.
- If children put their hands up or stand up when it isn't their number, they lose a point.

Extension activity

- Practise all the classroom language in the Welcome Topic.

1 My friends

In this topic pupils:
- greet another person and introduce themselves by name (Lesson 1)
- name classroom objects (Lessons 2, 3, 6 and 7)
- count from 1–10; recognise and name the numbers 1–10 (Lessons 5, 6, 8 and 12)
- name letters and exemplars *a–i*; match spoken sounds of *a–i* to written letters *a–i* (Lessons 4, 6, 7 and 10)
- ask and answer questions about objects and numbers (Lessons 7, 8, 9 and 11)
- follow and act out a simple story (Lesson 9)
- sing a short song (Lesson 10)
- write the letters *aA–gG* correctly (Lessons 1, 4, 5, 7, 9 and 11)
- write the numbers 1–6 (Lessons 2, 6 and 10).

Lesson 1

Performance indicators

Children will be able to:
- greet each other and introduce themselves by name
- recognise their own names written in English
- correctly name the four characters in the Pupil's Book
- write *a* and *A* correctly.

New language

Hello. I'm … .

Bring to the lesson

- the Tape
- the Flashcard for each of the course characters
- a name card for each character of the course
- a name card for each child in the class, and for yourself

Preparation

In addition to using the class name cards you produced in section one of the Welcome topic, you will need to prepare one name card for yourself and one each for Rania, Samir, Leila and Karim.

 page 10   **page 8**

Warm-up

- Say *Hello* to the whole class. Prompt the class to repeat. Do this as necessary until the class says it confidently.
- Go around the class. Say *Hello* to individuals. Elicit *Hello* in reply.

Presentation

Greeting someone

- Hold up your name card, point to yourself and say your name. Class repeats. Hold up a child's name card so the class can see it. Say the name. Give the card to the child and say, e.g. *Hello, Adam*. Prompt *Hello, Mr/Mrs/Miss (your name)*.

- When you have given a few cards out, prompt the class to join in saying *Hello, (child's name)*. Continue to prompt *Hello*, etc. in reply. Give out all the cards.

- Say *Hello, boys and girls* and indicate the whole class. Elicit from everyone *Hello, Mr/Mrs/Miss (your name)*.

Presenting the characters

- Hold up a character Flashcard and name card. Say the name. Prompt, e.g. *Hello, Rania*. Do the same with the other three.

- Hold up the Flashcards in any order without name cards. Class says the names. Stick the Flashcards on the board. Class names them. Stick up the name cards.

Introducing oneself

- Hold up your name card. Point to yourself and say *I'm Mr/Mrs/Miss (your name)*.

- Bring several children to the front, with their name cards. Stand them in a line facing the class. Stand on the right of the line (the class sees you on their left).

- Hold up your name card and say *I'm Mr/Mrs/Miss (your name)*. Prompt the child next to you to hold up his/her name card and say *I'm (his/her name)*. The other children in the line do the same. They sit down again.

- Prompt individuals around the class to hold up their name cards and say *I'm … .* Do the line activity again with different children saying *Hello, I'm … .*

page 10

1 Listen and point

- Hold up your book. Point to each character. Class says their names.

- Tell children to listen. Play the Tape. Point to Rania in your book as she speaks.

- Stop the Tape. Tell children to point in their books. Check they have the correct picture. Do the same as the other characters speak.

Tapescript

Narrator: Topic 1. My friends. Lesson 1. Activity 1. Listen and point.

Rania: Hello. I'm Rania.

Leila: Hello. I'm Leila.

Karim: Hello, Leila. I'm Karim.

Salama: Hello, boys and girls. I'm … .

- Play the Tape again straight through. Class points to the characters as they speak. Hold your book up. Point to each picture in turn and prompt the class to repeat what each character says.

2 Talk

- Bring forward three children with their name cards. Hold up your own name card. Say to the first child *Hello, I'm Mr/Mrs/Miss (your name)*. Prompt the reply *Hello, Mr/Mrs/Miss (your name), I'm* (e.g.) *Majid*. Repeat with the other two children.

- Bring four new children forward with their name cards. The first two face each other. Prompt one child to say, e.g. *Hello, I'm Mustafa*. The other replies *Hello, Mustafa. I'm Farida*. Do the same with the other two children.

- Children work in pairs. The first child holds up his/her name card says, e.g. Hello, *I'm Dina*. The second child holds up his/her card and replies *Hello, Dina. I'm … .* They do the activity again. The second child speaks first. Listen to some pairs.

Extension activity

- Bring four children forward. Mix up their name cards and put them on the board. Children find their own names. Repeat with another group of four. (*Variation*: the children must find another child's name and give it to him/her.)

page 8

1 Write

- To check correct letter formation, ask the class to stand up. Stand with your back to the class. Tell them to follow your action. Form the letter *a* in the air and check that they follow you accurately. Repeat with *A*.

- Children write over dotted lines inside the letter *a* next to the exemplar, following the arrrows in order.

- They write over the tinted letters *a* starting at the dot.

- They write over the smaller letters in the rows below, starting at the dot, then form the letter themselves.

- In the final row, children write letters independently, keeping within the guidelines.

- They write letter *A* in the same way.

- As children work, go around checking they are well positioned and holding the pencil correctly, as well as for correct letter formation.

Lesson 2

Performance indicators

Children will be able to:
- name classroom objects
- write *1* and *2* correctly.

New language

bag, book, pen, pencil

Review language

Greetings

Bring to the lesson

- the Tape
- the Flashcards for bag, book, pen and pencil
- a bag with a pen, a pencil, and a book inside

Preparation

Make sure all the children have brought into class a bag, a pen, a pencil and a book. In case any children haven't brought these items in, prepare in advance some pictures of these items to hand out.

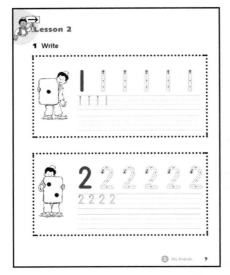

PB page 11   WB page 9

Warm-up

- Greet the class by saying *Hello, boys and girls*. Prompt *Hello, Mr/Mrs/Miss …* in reply.
- Greet a few children individually. Prompt the correct reply.

Presentation

Introducing objects

- Show the Flashcard for bag. Point and say *bag*. Class repeats. Do this until they speak confidently.
- Show another Flashcard and name it, e.g. *pencil*. Class repeats. Do this until they speak confidently.
- Introduce the third Flashcard in the same way.
- Hold up the three Flashcards in random order. Children say the words.
- Introduce the last object then revise all four.

PB page 11

1 Listen, find and say

- Children look in their books. Tell them to listen. Play the Tape.
- Hold up your book. Point to the pen as it is named. Tell the class to point. Check they have the correct picture. Prompt them to say the word in the pause.
- Continue with the other three words.

Tapescript

Narrator: Topic 1. Lesson 2. Activity 1. Listen, find and say.

Voice: Pen. [pause]

Bag. [pause]

Pencil. [pause]

Book. [pause]

- Play the Tape again, without stopping. Children listen, find the correct picture and say the word in the pause.

2 Play the game

- Make sure each child has a pen, a pencil and a book on his/her desk, and a bag. Alternatively, give out pictures of them. (Children hold them up when named.)

- Hold up each object and name it. Prompt the class to do the same.

- Put your bag on your desk and say *bag*. Say to the class *Point to your bag*.

- Hold up and name an object, e.g. *pencil*. Prompt the class to do the same. Check they have the correct object. Put your pencil in your bag. Class does the same.

- Repeat with the other two objects.

- For more practice, repeat the activity, this time prompting the class to take the objects out of their bags.

Extension activities

Play team games with the class divided into two.

- Name an object, the class holds it up. The first team to be all sitting still, holding up the correct object, wins a point.

- Hold up the four different objects in random order. The first team to name an object correctly wins a point.

 page 9

1 Write

For detailed guidance notes on handwriting practice, see the teaching notes on page 19 (Workbook, Lesson 1, Activity 1).

- Children write over the arrowed lines in the number *1*s, starting at the dot.

- They write over the tinted numbers, starting at the dot.

- They then complete the row writing numbers independently.

- They do the same with the number *2*.

Lesson 3

Performance indicators

Children will be able to:
- follow the instruction *Find*
- name four new classroom objects
- recognise differences in pictures.

New language

crayon, pencil case, rubber, ruler

Review language

book, bag, pencil, pen

Bring to the lesson

- the Tape
- a pencil case with a rubber, a ruler and a crayon inside
- a pen, a pencil, a book and a bag

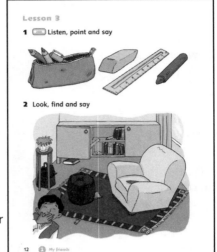

PB **page 12** WB **page 10**

Warm-up

- Greet the class with *Hello, boys and girls*. Prompt *Hello, Mr/Mrs/Miss ...* .

- Say to a child, *Hello, I'm Mr/Mrs/Miss ...* . Prompt, e.g. *Hello, Mr/Mrs/Miss ... . I'm Mona*. Repeat with other individuals.

- Stand four children in a line facing the class. Say to the first child *Hello, I'm Mr/Mrs/Miss ...* . Prompt the reply *Hello, Mr/Mrs/Miss ... . I'm ...* .

- The first child says to the second, e.g. *Hello, I'm Nadine*. The second replies, *Hello, Nadine. I'm Samir*, and so on to the end of the line.

- Do the activity again with other children.

Presentation

- Show the class a pencil case. Point and say *pencil case*. Class repeats. Do this until they speak confidently.

- Open your pencil case and take out one of the other objects. Show it and name it, e.g. *rubber*. Class repeats. Do this until they speak confidently.

- Introduce the third object in the same way.

- Hold up the three objects in any order. Children say the words.

- Introduce the last object then revise all four.

Optional Develop the words into a simple chant. Point to each object in turn using a regular rhythm. Bring a child to the front to point to the objects. The rest of the class says the word in the rhythm. You could encourage them to clap as they say each word.

PB **page 12**

1 Listen, point and say

- Children look at the pictures for a minute or two. Tell them to listen and point to the objects named. Play the Tape.

- Children point and repeat the words in the pauses.

Tapescript

Narrator: Topic 1. Lesson 3. Activity 1. Listen, point and say.

Voice: Pencil case. [pause]

Rubber. [pause]

Ruler. [pause]

Crayon. [pause]

- Play the Tape again. Children repeat in the pauses. (Alternatively, hold up each object and say the words yourself.) Class repeats until they speak confidently.

2 Look, find and say

- Hold up the real objects to revise *pen*, *pencil*, *book* and *bag*. Class names them.

- Teach or revise *Find*. Place a few classroom objects under a cloth or in a box. Say to individuals, e.g. *Dina, find the crayon, please*.

- Children look at the picture in their books. Explain that Salama has hidden objects in the room and they must find them. Say *Find the book*.

- Children look and say the word when they have found the object. Children should also find a bag, a pen, a pencil case, a ruler, a pencil, a rubber and a crayon.

Extension activity

- Place all eight classroom objects on your desk. Children take turns to come out and hold up an object. Class names them.

 page 10

1 Circle the odd one out

- Children look at the first row. Point out Salama drawing a circle round the last pencil. Say *It's different*. Ask children to explain why (it is pointing the other way).

- Children look at the three rows and circle the object that is different in each one.

- If you wish, let children say why the circled objects are different, but do not try to teach the explanation in English. The purpose of this exercise is simply for children to notice the difference.

2 Find, join and say

- Children look at the objects outside the picture then find them in the picture.

- Say, e.g. *bag*. Demonstrate drawing a line between the bag on the outside and the bag in the picture. Children draw the line. Check their work. They point and name the object.

- Children draw the other lines. Check their work. They point and name the objects.

Lesson 4

Performance indicators

Children will be able to:
- recognise and name the letters *a*, *b* and *c*
- match phonic sounds /æ/,/b/ and /k/ to written letters *a*, *b* and *c*
- name three new objects
- write *b* and *B* correctly.

New language

apple, ball, cat

Review language

bag, book, pen, pencil, pencil case, rubber, crayon, ruler

Bring to the lesson

- the Tape
- the alphabet Flashcards for a, b and c
- real classroom objects (for review)
- small picture cards of classroom objects (bag, book, pen, pencil)
- small picture cards for a, b and c exemplars (apple, book and cat)

Preparation

Use the Resources pages 162–167 to make enough of the apple, ball and cat exemplar picture cards, and of the classroom object picture cards (bag, book, pencil, pen), for all of the children in the class to have three or four different cards each. If you wish, you could make picture cards for the additional vocabulary items too (pencil case, crayon, ruler, rubber). See page 162 for preparation instructions.

PB **page 13**   WB **page 11**

Warm-up

- Greet the class with *Hello, boys and girls*. Elicit *Hello, Mr/Mrs/Miss … .*
- Revise the classroom objects. Hold up each one and ask the class to name it.

- Show the letter. Say *a* and the sound, /æ/. Show the picture. Say *apple*. Show them again. Class says *a*, /æ/, *apple*.
- Do the same with the *b* and *c* Flashcards.

Presentation

Note: The Welcome topic revised/introduced the names of letters. If children are already familiar with the sounds of letters, take the Presentation section and Activity 1 at a faster pace to suit the class.

- Hold up the alphabet Flashcard for the letter *a*, with the picture showing. Say *apple*. Class repeats. Turn the card to show the letter *a*. Class names it

PB **page 13**

1 Listen, look and say

- Children look at the three pictures for a moment.
- Tell them to look at the first letter and picture and listen. Play the sequence for *a* on the Tape. Children repeat in the pauses. Stop the Tape.

- Point to the apple in the book. Prompt children to point. Check they have the correct picture. Say *a, /æ/, apple*. Children repeat.

- Follow the procedure in the same way for *b* and *c*.

- Play the Tape without stopping. Children point in their books and repeat in the pauses.

Tapescript

Narrator: Topic 1. Lesson 4. Activity 1.

Voice: a. [pause] /æ/. [pause] Apple. [pause]

b. [pause] /b/. [pause] Ball. [pause]

c. [pause] /k/. [pause] Cat. [pause]

2 Play the picture game

- Hold up your book. Point to each child character in turn. Class names them.

- Point to each object in the first row. Class names them. Do the same with the other two rows. Point to objects in any row. Class names them.

- Point out Salama with his pencil. Tell the children to pick up their pencils.

- Say, e.g. *Rania* and point to the row of objects next to the character. Name one of them, e.g. *Rania's bag*. Demonstrate to the children how to look along the row, find the bag and circle it.

- If necessary, demonstrate again using other rows, then begin the game. You may wish to make up your own sequence or you can follow this one: *Rania's pen; Karim's book; Leila's bag; Rania's bag: Karim's pen; Leila's pencil.*

- When you have called out two objects from each row, check a few children's books.

Extension activities

- Ask children to say which object in each row has not been circled. If you used the sequence above, the answers are: Rania's pencil, Karim's bag, Leila's book. Play the *Name the object game*.

- Give out small picture cards of classroom objects and small picture cards for the *a, b* and *c* alphabet exemplars so that each child has three or four cards. Name an object. The children who have that picture hold it up and repeat the word. Whole class repeats.

 page 11

1 Write

For detailed guidance notes on handwriting practice, see the teaching notes on page 19 (Workbook, Lesson 1, Activity 1).

- Children write over the dotted lines inside the letter *b* next to the exemplar, following the arrows in order.

- They write over the tinted letters *b* starting at the dot.

- They complete the rows starting at the dot.

- They write a row independently, keeping within the guidelines.

- They do the same for the letter *B*.

Lesson 5

Performance indicators

Children will be able to:
- recognise and say the numbers 1–5
- count up to 5
- write *c* and *C* correctly.

New language

1, 2, 3, 4, 5

Review language

apple, ball, cat

Bring to the lesson

- the Tape
- the Flashcards for numbers 1–5
- the Flashcards for apple, ball and cat (for review)

PB **page 14**   WB **page 12**

Warm-up

- Greet the class with *Hello, boys and girls.* Prompt *Hello, Mr/Mrs/Miss … .*

- Briefly revise *apple, ball and cat.* Show the Flashcards in abc order. Class names them. Show them in any order. Class names them. Ask some individuals.

- Show the letters on the other side. Prompt children to name them and say the sounds: a /æ/, b /b/, c /k/.

Presentation

Note: If children are already familiar with the numbers 1–5, take this lesson at a faster pace to suit your class.

- Hold up the first number Flashcard and say *1.* The class repeats until they speak confidently.

- Do the same with the other Flashcards.

PB **page 14**

 1 Listen, point and say

- Children look at the numbers for a moment or two.

- Play the first part of the Tape. Hold up your book and point to each number. Prompt children to point in their own books and repeat in the pauses.

Tapescript

Narrator: Topic 1. Lesson 5. Activity 1. Listen, point and say.

Voice: 1. [pause]

2. [pause]

3. [pause]

4. [pause]

5. [pause]

- Play the Tape again (or say each number yourself). Class repeats. Check that children are pointing to the correct number each time.

- Hold up number Flashcards one by one in order and say them. Class repeats.

- Put the Flashcards on the board in order. Point in order. Children say the numbers.

- Tell children to look at you and listen. Play the Tape. Children repeat in the pauses. Check pronunciation.

Tapescript

Narrator: Now listen again and say the numbers.

Voice: 1 (one beat). [pause]

2 (two beats). [pause]

3 (three beats). [pause]

4 (four beats). [pause]

5 (five beats). [pause]

2 Play the game

- Put the Flashcards 1–5 face down in a pile on your desk. A child comes forward, chooses a Flashcard and shows the number to the rest of the class.

- Prompt the class to count up to it, clapping as they say each number.

- Continue with other children choosing a Flashcard.

- Vary the activity:

1 Pairs of children come out. One chooses a Flashcard, the other claps and counts.

2 Divide the class into two teams. Hold up a Flashcard for each team in turn. The whole team must clap and count together. If they can do it, they get a point. If they get stuck, help them to do it correctly.

Extension activity

- Bring five confident children to the front. Give out the Flashcards 1–5 in order. Clap your hands, e.g. twice. The child holding number 2 holds up the card.

- The whole class claps and counts to two. Repeat with other numbers.

- As a variation, let different children in the class clap their hands for a number to be held up.

 page 12

1 Write

For detailed guidance notes on handwriting practice, see the teaching notes on page 19 (Workbook, Lesson 1, Activity 1).

- Children write over the dotted lines inside the letter *c* next to the exemplar, following the arrows in order.

- They write over the tinted letters *c* starting at the dot.

- They complete the rows starting at the dot.

- They write a row independently, keeping within the guidelines.

- They do the same for the letter *C*.

Lesson 6

Performance indicators

Children will be able to:
- recognise and say the numbers 1–5
- name objects
- count objects up to 5
- write 3 and 4 correctly.

Review language

1, 2, 3, 4, 5
pen, apple, ball, bag, cat

Bring to the lesson

- the Flashcards for pen, apple, ball, bag and cat
- the Flashcards for numbers 1–5

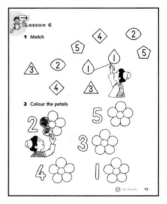

 page 15   **pages 13 and 14**

Warm-up

- Greet the class in the usual way.
- Revise the numbers 1–5. Hold the Flashcards up one by one in order. Class says the number. Hold them up in any order. Class says the number

Presentation

- Put the number Flashcards 1–5 on the board with the pen, apple, ball, bag and cat Flashcards below them.
- Point to a number. Class names it. Point to the picture. Class names the object.
- Change the order of the picture cards. Repeat the activity.

 page 15

1 Play the Flashcard game

- Give children a moment or two to look at the page.
- Ask a child to point to a number and say it. Ask another child to name the object next to it.

- Repeat with other pairs across the class.
- Children work in pairs taking turns to say a number then name the object.

Extension activity

Play the *Flashcard numbers and pictures game*.

- Put the Flashcards 1–5 on the board. Put up different picture Flashcards by each number. Divide the class into teams. A child from team A says a number. A child from team B names the object.
- Then it is a child from team B's turn to say a number. A child from team A names the object.
- Change the Flashcards and play again.

 pages 13 and 14

1 Match

- Point out how Salama is joining two numbers which

are the same.

- Children look for other numbers that match and draw lines between them.

- Go round checking as they work. Encourage them to draw from left to right.

2 Colour the petals

- Children look at the numbers and colour in the correct number of petals.

3 Write

For detailed guidance notes on handwriting practice, see the teaching notes on page 19 (Workbook, Lesson 1, Activity 1).

- Children write over the arrowed lines in the number 3s, starting at the dot.

- They then trace the tinted numbers, starting at the dot.

- They then complete the row writing figures independently.

- They do the same with the number 4.

Lesson 7

Performance indicators

Children will be able to:
- ask and answer questions about an object
- recognise and name the letters *d, e* and *f*
- match phonic sounds /d /, /ɛ/ and /f/ to written letters *d, e* and *f*
- write *d* and *D* correctly.

New language

What is it?
It's a ...
dog, egg, fan

Review language

ball, book, cat, pencil, pencil case, apple, pen, rubber, ruler

Bring to the lesson
- the Tape
- real classroom objects from Lessons 2 and 3
- the Flashcards for apple, ball, cat, dog, egg and fan

PB **page 16**   **WB** **page 15**

Warm-up
- Greet the class in the usual way.
- Hold up classroom items and Flashcards of objects the children can name. Class names them.

Presentation
- Introduce the new question and answer. Hold up, e.g. a book. Ask *What is it?* Say, *It's a book.* Class repeats the answer. Ask again; prompt the answer again.
- Ask and prompt answers using a pencil, pencil case and the cat and dog Flashcards.

 page 16

 1 Listen and find
- Tell children to look at the pictures and listen for the sound of each object.
- Play the first part of the Tape.

Tapescript

Narrator: Topic 1. Lesson 7. Activity 1. Listen and find.

Sound effect: [cat miaowing]

Karim: What is it?

Rania: It's a cat.

Sound effect: [ball bouncing]

Karim: What is it?

Rania: It's a ... . Oh! It's a ball.

Sound effect: [pencil case being undone]

Karim: What is it?

Rania: It's a ... a ... . Oh! It's a pencil case.

Sound effect: [pencil drawing/writing on paper]

Karim: What is it?

Rania:	Oh! It's a pencil.
Sound effect:	[book pages being turned and snap of book shutting]
Karim:	What is it?
Rania:	It's a ... a ... . Oh! It's a book.
Karim:	Good! Well done!

- Children listen and look at the pictures in their books. Play the rest of the Tape.
- Prompt them to point to the correct picture and answer in the pause. You may need to help them with the first one or two. Play the Tape twice, if necessary.

Tapescript

Narrator:	Now listen and say.
Sound effect:	[cat miaowing]
Voice:	What is it? [pause]
Sound effect:	[ball bouncing]
Voice:	What is it? [pause]
Sound effect:	[pencil case being undone]
Voice:	What is it? [pause]
Sound effect:	[pencil drawing/writing on paper]
Voice:	What is it? [pause]
Sound effect:	[book's pages being turned and snap of book shutting]
Voice:	What is it? [pause]
Voice:	Good! Well done!

- Practise *What is it?* with two children at the front of the class. Show the ball Flashcard to the first child. Ask *What is it?* Elicit *It's a ball.* Give him/her the Flashcard.
- Prompt him/her to show the ball Flashcard to the second child and ask *What is it?* The second child answers.
- Repeat with two or three other pairs and Flashcards.
- Divide the class in two. Give an object to a child on one side who holds it up. All children on that side ask *What is it?* All children on the other side answer.
- The second side now asks the question, holding up a different Flashcard or object.
- Repeat until the whole class asks confidently. To check, give individuals a Flashcard or object and prompt the question. A child or the whole class answers.

2 Listen, look and say

- Hold up the alphabet Flashcard for the letter *d*, with the picture showing. Say *dog*. Class repeats. Turn the card to show the letter *d*. Class names it.
- Show the letter. Say *d* /d/. Show the picture. Say *Dog*. Show them again. Class says *d, /d/, dog*.
- Do the same with the *e* and *f* Flashcards.
- Children look in their books at the three pictures. Tell them to listen and look at the first letter and picture. Play the sequence for *d* on the Tape. Stop the Tape.
- Point to the dog in the book. Prompt children to point. Check they have the correct picture. Say *d, /d/, dog*. Children repeat.
- Follow the procedure in the same way for *e* and *f*.
- Play the Tape again without stopping. Children point in their books and repeat the sounds and words.

Tapescript

Narrator:	Topic 1. Lesson 7. Activity 2. Listen, look and say.
Voice:	d. [pause] /d/. [pause] Dog. [pause]
	e. [pause] /ɜ/. [pause] Egg. [pause]
	f. [pause] /f/. [pause] Fan. [pause]

Extension activity

- Put all or some of these into a bag: a book, a pen, a pencil, a ruler, a rubber, Flashcards for apple, ball, cat, dog and fan. Children take turns to come to the front, take something from the bag, show it to the rest of the class and ask *What is it*. Class answers.

 page 15

1 Write

For detailed guidance notes on handwriting practice, see the teaching notes on page 19 (Workbook, Lesson 1, Activity 1).

- Children write over the dotted lines inside the letter *d* next to the exemplar, following the arrows in order.
- They then write over the tinted letters *d* starting at the dot and complete the rows starting at the dot.
- They write a row independently, keeping within the guidelines.
- They do the same for the letter *D*.

Lesson 8

Performance indicators

Children will be able to:
- recognise and say the numbers 6–10
- count objects up to ten
- ask a question about numbers.

New language

6, 7, 8, 9, 10
What number is it?

Review language

1, 2, 3, 4, 5

Bring to the lesson

- the Tape
- the Flashcards for numbers 1–10
- Flashcard-sized dotted cards for numbers 1–10

Preparation

You will nedd to make a set of 10 Flashcard-sized dotted cards for the numbers 1–10. See page 162 for preparation instructions.

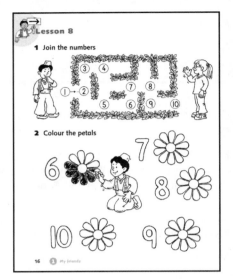

PB **page 17**   WB **page 16**

Warm-up

- Greet the class in the usual way.
- Revise the numbers 1–5. Hold up the Flashcards one by one in order. Children say the numbers.
- Put them on the board. Point in any order. Children say the numbers.
- Call out a number. The whole class claps and counts to that number.

Presentation

- Teach the word *number*. Show the number *1* Flashcard. Say *number*. Point to 1. Say *number 1*.
- Show the next Flashcard. Say *number*. Point to 2. Say *Number 2*.
- Repeat with the numbers 3–5.

PB **page 17**

1 Listen, point and say

- Introduce the numbers as in Lesson 5. Hold up the number 6 Flashcard. Say 6. Class repeats until they speak confidently. Do the same with the number Flashcards for 7–10.
- Children look at the numbers on page 17 for a moment or two.
- Play the first part of the Tape. Hold up your book and point to each number as it is mentioned. Prompt children to point in their books and repeat in the pause.

Tapescript

Narrator: Topic 1. Lesson 8. Activity 1. Listen, point and say.

Voice: 6. [pause]

7. [pause]

8. [pause]

9. [pause]

10. [pause]

- Play the Tape again (or say each number yourself). Class repeats. Check that children point to the correct number in their books.

- Hold up the Flashcards for 6–10 one by one in order. Say the number. Class repeats.

- Put them on the board in order. Point to numbers in any order, children say them.

- Play the Tape. Children listen to the beats and repeat in the pauses.

Tapescript

Narrator: Now listen again and say the numbers.

Voice: 6 (six beats). [pause]

7 (seven beats). [pause]

8 (eight beats). [pause]

9 (nine beats). [pause]

10 (ten beats). [pause]

- Practise the numbers 6–10 with Flashcard activities:

1 A child takes a Flashcard from the pile on your desk and holds the card up to the class. The class claps and counts.

2 Five children take turns to hold up Flashcards and say the numbers. Class claps and counts. This can also be done with the class in teams.

2 Point and talk

- Give out the Flashcards 2–10. Put up number 1 on the board. Point to the space beside it. Prompt 2. The child with the number 2 Flashcard puts it next to the number 1. Continue until all ten cards are placed in the correct order.

- Point to numbers in random order. Ask *What number is it?* Class answers.

- Children look in their books at the dotted cards. Hold up your book. Point to each card in turn. Class counts the dots on that card in their books.

- Bring 10 children forward. Give out the large dotted cards in order. Children hold up cards in turn and ask *What number is it?* Class answers.

Extension activities

- Stick the number Flashcards 1–10 on the board in order. Give out the large dotted cards. In any order, children put their dotted card under the correct number Flashcard.

- Class checks by counting the dots as you point. If the Flashcard and dotted number card match, class can say *Good! Well done.* If they do not, help the child do it correctly.

 page 16

1 Join the numbers

- Children draw over the dotted line between the numbers, starting at 1. They draw the missing connecting lines.

2 Colour the petals

- Children look at the numbers and colour the correct number of petals on each flower.

Lesson 9

Performance indicators

Children will be able to:
- name objects from Lessons 1–8
- ask and answer questions about objects
- write e and E correctly.

Review language

bag, ball, book, cat, dog, fan, pen, pencil, pencil case, crayon, rubber, ruler
What is it? It's a … .

Bring to the lesson

- the Tape
- Flashcards for numbers 1–5
- the Flashcards for ball, cat, dog, fan, book, bag, pen and pencil.
- 5 or 6 sets of 8 picture card to match the Flashcards above.

Preparation

You will need to make enough sets of 8 picture cards (ball, cat, dog, fan, book, bag, pen and pencil) for each child to have two cards (See Extension activity). For preparation instructions see pages 162–167.

PB **page 18**   WB **page 17**

Warm-up

- Greet the class in the usual way.

- Revise the numbers 1–5:
  1 Hold up the number Flashcards in any order. Ask *What number is it?* Class answers.
  2 Class says numbers 1–5 in order.
  3 Children say numbers 1–5 round the class: the first child says *1*, the second child says *2*, etc.

Presentation

- Use the course character Flashcards to revise their names.

- Use classroom objects to practise *Find*. Put items in a box or under a cloth. Say, e.g. *Mona, find the ruler, please*. When the child has the object, he/she holds it up. Ask the class *What is it?* Class replies *It's a ruler*.

- Do this a few times with different children and different objects.

PB **page 18**

1 Listen and read

- Let children look at the pictures in their books for a moment or two.

- Say *Find the pencil case*. Children look and point in their books. Do the same with the ruler and the crayon.

- Ask children to say what they think is happening in the story. Samir has hidden some items for Karim to find. Rania was sitting on the crayon.

- Tell children to listen and look in their books. Play the Tape. Children follow the story in the pictures.

Tapescript

Narrator: Topic 1. Lesson 9. Activity 1. Listen and read.

Samir: Find the pencil case.

Karim: Here it is!

Samir: Find the ruler.

Karim:	Here it is!
Samir:	Find the crayon.
Rania:	Samir! Look!
Samir:	Oh, dear!

- Read the speech bubbles aloud one at a time. Class repeats. Do this again, if necessary.

- Practise the language with the class in two teams. Put a pencil case, a ruler and a crayon around the classroom. Prompt a child on team A to give an instruction, e.g. *Find the crayon*. All the children on that team repeat.

- Choose a child from the Team B to find it. The child holds up the crayon. The whole team says *Here it is*. Do this a few times, adding in new objects. Then change over and team B gives the instruction.

- Play the Tape again. Children listen and follow.

2 Act it out

- Divide the class into three groups and assign a character to each group. Children say the words for their character together.

- Groups change characters and say their parts again.

- Let some children come forward in threes to act out the story to the class, each one saying the words of a different character.

Extension activity

- Divide the class into groups of four. Give each group a set of 8 picture cards (ball, cat, dog, fan, bag, book, pencil, pen). The cards are divided among the members of the group so that each child has two cards. Place the Flashcards that match the small cards on your desk.

- Select a Flashcard (but do not show it) and say, e.g. *Find the dog*. The child in each group who has the dog picture card shows it and says *Here it is*. Show the Flashcard to the class. Ask *What is it?* Class answers *It's a dog*.

- Repeat with different Flashcards.

 page 17

1 Write

For detailed guidance notes on handwriting practice, see the teaching notes on page 19 (Workbook, Lesson 1, Activity 1).

- Children write over the dotted lines inside the letter *e* next to the exemplar, following the arrows in order.

- They write over the tinted letters *e* starting at the dot.

- They complete the rows starting at the dot.

- They write a row independently, keeping within the guidelines.

- They do the same for the letter *E*.

Lesson 10

Performance indicators

Children will be able to:
- sing a four-line song
- give a formal greeting
- recognise and name the letters *g*, *h* and *i*
- match phonic sounds /g/, /h/ and /ɪ/ to written letters, *g*, *h* and *i*
- write the numbers 5 and 6 correctly.

New language

Good morning.
goat, hand, insect

Review language

book, bag, pen, pencil, apple, ball,
cat, dog, egg, fan
6, 7, 8, 9, 10

Bring to the lesson

- the Tape
- real classroom objects or Flashcards
- the Flashcards for 6–10
- the Flashcards for goat, hand and insect

PB **page 19**   WB **page 18**

Warm-up

- Greet the class in the usual way.
- Hold up real objects and Flashcards to prompt the review vocabulary.
- Use number Flashcards to revise the numbers 6–10. Ask the class and individuals *What number is it?* Say *Good! Well done!* as appropriate during this revision session.

Presentation

- Say *Hello*. Prompt the class to repeat.
- Say *Good morning*. Class repeats.
- Say to individuals, e.g. *Good morning, Hassan.* Children reply *Good morning, Mr/Mrs/Miss … .*
- Say *Hello* and *Good morning*. Class repeats.

PB **page 19**

1 Sing

- Class looks at the pictures on page 19. Point to the girls on the left in your book. Wave and say *Hello* and *Good morning*. Do the same with the boys on the right.
- Play the Tape. Let children listen and look at the pictures in their books.

Tapescript

Narrator: Topic 1. Lesson 10. Activity 1. Sing.

Group 1: Hello and good morning,

Good morning to you.

Group 2: Hello and good morning,

Good morning to you.

- Say the first line and add a waving action. Class repeats and waves. Say the second line with a different action, e.g. one or both hands in a welcoming gesture.

- Prompt the class to say both lines together with actions.

- Play the Tape again. Class sings along.

- Divide the class in two. Each side sings two lines to the other, with or without the Tape.

2 Listen, look and say

- Hold up the alphabet Flashcard for the letter *g*, with the picture showing. Say *goat*. Class repeats. Turn the card to show the letter *g*. Class names it.

- Show the letter. Say *g*, /g/. Show the picture. Say *goat*. Show them again. Class says *g*, /g/, *goat*.

- Do the same with the *h* and *i* Flashcards.

- Children look in their books. Tell them to listen and look at the first letter and picture.

- Play the sequence for *g* on the Tape. Pause it. Point to the goat in the book. Prompt children to point. Check they have the correct picture. Say *g*, /g/, *goat*. Children repeat.

- Follow the procedure in the same way for *h* and *i*.

- Play the Tape without stopping. Children point in their books and repeat.

Tapescript

Narrator: topic 1. Lesson 10. Activity 2. Listen, look and say.

Voice: g. [pause] /g/. [pause] Goat. [pause]

 h. [pause] /h/. [pause] Hand. [pause]

 i. [pause] /ɪ/. [pause] Insect. [pause]

---

 page 18

1 Write

For detailed guidance notes on handwriting practice, see the teaching notes on page 19 (Workbook, Lesson 1, Activity 1).

- Children write over the arrowed lines in the number 5s, starting at the dot and following the numbered arrows.

- They write over the tinted numbers in the same way, then write independently.

- They do the same with the number 6.

Extension activities

- Sing the song from Activity 1 again, dividing the class up in different ways, e.g. boys and girls or rows.

- Practise *Good morning* as a greeting. Say *Good morning, boys and girls*. Prompt *Good morning, Mr/Mrs/Miss …* . Practise with individuals.

- At the end of the lesson introduce *Goodbye*. Get ready to leave, tell the children to stand up, etc., then say *Goodbye* and prompt the class to repeat. Say *Goodbye, boys and girl*. Prompt the response *Goodbye, Mr/Mrs/Miss …* .

Lesson 11 – Review

Performance indicators

Children will be able to:
- use and understand the language taught in Lessons 1–10
- write *f* and *F* correctly
- write *g* and *G* correctly

Review

Words and structures in Topic 1

Bring to the lesson

- the Tape
- the Flashcards for numbers 1–10
- real classroom objects or Flashcards

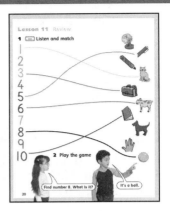

PB **page 20**   WB **page 19 and 20**

Warm-up

- Greet the class with *Good morning, boys and girls* and elicit the correct response. From now on, use this greeting at the start of your lessons.

- Do some activities to revise all the words and structures learnt so far. For example:

Words and questions
- Hold up real items or Flashcards of all objects taught so far. Children name them.

- Hold up real items or Flashcards and ask *What is it?* Elicit *It's a ... .* (Leave out *apple, egg* and *insect* as *an* hasn't been taught yet.)

Numbers
- Children say numbers round the class, 1–10, in sequence.

- Hold up number Flashcards in random order. Ask *What number is it?* Class answers.

Presentation

- Revise *Find*. Put up the number Flashcards on the board. Bring several children to the front.

- Instruct each child, e.g., *Maged, find number 6.* Prompt each child to look, find and point to the correct number.

PB **page 20**

1 Listen and match

- Children look at page 20 for a moment or two.

- Say *Find number 1.* Hold up your book and follow the line from 1 to the cat. Children follow the line in their books.

- Point and ask *What is it?* Elicit *It's a cat.* Repeat with numbers 3, 5, 6, 8 and 10.

- Tell the children to listen. Play the first line of the Tape then pause it. Hold up your book. Point to number 2. Repeat *Number 2 is a fan.* Indicate the pictures on the right. Say *Find the fan.* Check that children point to the correct picture.

- Go through the same procedure with numbers 4, 7 and 9.

- Say *Number 2 is a fan*. Demonstrate drawing a line from number 2 to the fan.

- Tell children to listen and be ready to draw lines between the numbers and objects they hear.

- Play the Tape again. Stop it, if necessary, to help or check the children's work.

Tapescript

Narrator: Topic 1. Lesson 11. Activity 1. Listen and match.

Child 1: Number 2 is a fan. [pause]

Child 2: Number 4 is a hand. [pause]

Child 3: Number 7 is a pencil. [pause]

Child 4: Number 9 is a dog. [pause]

---

2 Play the game

- Hold up your book. Say *Find number 8*. Children point to number 8 in their books. Ask *What is it?* Children follow the line to the object. Prompt *It's a ball*.

- Repeat with two or three other numbers.

- Let a child choose a number Flashcard from your desk without showing the class. Prompt the child to say, e.g. *Find number 2. What is it?*

- Tell children to put their hands up when they have found the object. Elicit the answer chorally from the whole class.

- Repeat with other children choosing a number and asking.

Extension activities

You may also wish to do a short individual oral/aural check on other aspects of the work covered, for example:

- Show objects/pictures/numbers and elicit answers to *What is it?/What number is it?*

- Ask children to count to a given number.

- Ask children to respond to *Hello. I'm ... . / Good morning, ...*

 page 19 and 20

1 Write

For detailed guidance notes on handwriting practice, see the teaching notes on page 19 (Workbook, Lesson 1, Activity 1).

- Children write over the dotted lines inside the letter *f* next to the exemplar, following the arrows in order.

- They trace over the tinted letters *f* starting at the dot.

- They complete the rows starting at the dot.

- They write a row independently, keeping within the guidelines.

- They do the same for the letter *F*.

2 Write

- Children practise writing *g* and *G* as in Activity 1, above.

Lesson 12

Performance indicators

Children will be able to.
- say and recognise the numbers 1–10
- name letters
- recognise initial letters
- write letters *a–g*
- listen to and follow instructions.

Review

Numbers *1–10*

Bring to the lesson

- the Flashcards for numbers 1–10
- small number cards 1–10
- small dotted cards

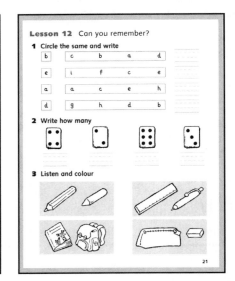

Preparation

- Make enough small number cards for each child in the class to have one card. See page 162 for preparation instructions.
- Make enough small dotted number cards for each child in the class to have one card. These should look the same as the large dotted cards that you made in Lesson 8, but the same size as normal number or picture cards. See page 162 for preparation instructions.

PB **page 21** WB **page 21**

Warm-up

- Children sing the song *Hello and good morning* from Lesson 10, Activity 1.

- Divide the class in two. One half sings the first two lines, the other half replies with the second two.

- Divide the class into smaller groups. Each group sings two lines to the next group.

Presentation

- Choose ten children to come out and hold the number Flashcards. Give out the Flashcards in order.

- They hold up their Flashcards. Class says numbers 1–10 together.

- Tell every second child to turn their Flashcards so the blank side faces the class. Point to each card in sequence starting from 1. Class counts together and says the numbers of the missing number Flashcards.

- *Alternative*: mix up the children in the line. The class then calls out *Number 1*. The child with this Flashcard moves to the left of the line and steps forward. The class then continues calling out numbers in order until all the children are lined up correctly.

 page 21

1 Play the Flashcard game

- Choose ten new children to hold the number Flashcards. Give out the Flashcards in any order.

- Ask the class to count slowly to 10. See if the new group can line up in the correct order by the time the class reaches number 10.

- Tell the class to look in their books at page 21. Tell the children with Flashcards to turn their numbers face down. Call out the name of one of the children in the line. This child holds up his/her Flashcard. The other children in the class point to the number in their books and say it.

Extension activities

- Give out a small number card to each child. Say a number. Children with that number stand up and show their number. Children change numbers and play again.

- Divide the class into small groups. Give each group four or five dotted cards and the matching number cards. Mix the cards up and put them face down. Children turn them up and match up the numbers with the dotted cards. The first group to finish correctly wins a point. Groups change sets and play again.

Note: You can also play this game matching capital and small letters. See page 162 for instructions on preparing letter cards. These number and letter sets can also be used for pairs of slower children who need extra practice, or for individuals.

 page 21

- If you wish, you may use page 21 as a test to check on class progress. If you do this, prepare examples of the first two exercises to do on the board with the whole class to ensure that they understand these tasks. Then let them do the first two tasks independently. Give them a fixed length of time to complete them.

- For the third exercise explain that they must listen and colour the object you name out of each pair.

- Alternatively, you can use this page as normal Workbook exercises and explain each task in turn, keeping the whole class working together.

1 Circle the same and write

- Children look at each line of letters and identify the two which are the same. They circle them and write the letter in the grid on the right.

2 Write how many

- Children count the dots on each card and write the number in the grid underneath.

Answers

4, 2, 6, 3

3 Listen and colour

- Children listen and colour whichever of the two objects they hear named in each pair of pictures. You may choose yourself which of the two words you say.

② My class

In this topic pupils:

- ask someone their name (Lesson 1)
- ask someone their age and give their own age (Lesson 2)
- give and follow a simple instruction (Lesson 3)
- name four new classroom items (Lesson 3)
- name letters and exemplars *j–r* (Lessons 4, 7 and 10)
- match phonic sounds to written letters *j–r* (Lessons 4, 7 and 10)

- name the colours blue, green and yellow (Lesson 5), and red, black and white (Lesson 7)
- describe objects by colour (Lessons 8 and 9)
- act out a story (Lesson 9)
- sing a song (Lesson 10)
- write letters *hH–pP* correctly (Lessons 2, 4, 5, 6, 7, 8, 10 and 11)
- write the numbers 7–10 (Lessons 1 and 3)
- practise and consolidate (Lessons 3, 6, 9, 11 and 12)

Lesson 1

Performance indicators

Children will be able to:
- ask someone their name
- give their own name when asked
- write *7* and *8* correctly.

New language

name
What's your name?

Review language

What is it?
What number is it?
Good morning/Hello, I'm … .

Bring to the lesson

- the Tape
- the course character Flashcards
- a few Flashcards for the Warm-up activities
- the Flashcards 1–10

PB **page 22**   WB **page 22**

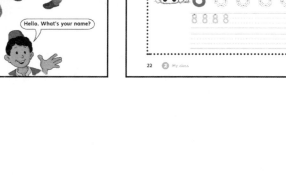

Warm-up

- Greet the class with *Good morning, boys and girls.* Prompt the correct reply.

- Hold up Flashcards of objects one by one. Ask *What is it?* Class replies.

- Hold up number Flashcards. Ask *What number is it?* Class replies.

- Hold up different Flaschards at random and get individuals to answer questions.

Presentation

- Say to a child *Hello, I'm Mr/Mrs/Miss … .* Prompt *Hello, Mr/Mrs/Miss … . I'm … .* Do this a few times with other children.

- Write your name on the board. Say *Name.* Class repeats.

- Say to several children *Hello. What's your name?* Prompt, e.g. *I'm Ali.*

 page 22

 1 Listen and point

- Hold up the course character Flashcards in turn. Children name them.

- Tell the class to listen with their books closed. Play the Tape. Hold up the correct Flashcard as each character says his/her name.

Tapescript

Narrator:	Topic 2. My class. Lesson 1. Activity 1. Listen and point.
Child:	Hello. What's your name?
Karim:	I'm Karim.
Karim:	Hello. What's your name?
Leila:	I'm Leila.
Leila:	Hello. What's your name?
Samir:	I'm Samir.
Samir:	Hello. What's your name?
Rania:	Good morning, Samir. I'm Rania, of course!

- Tell children to look in their books and point to the characters when they say their names. Play the Tape again. Check that children point to the correct character.

- Play the Tape again or read out the Tapescript. Stop after each question. Class repeats.

2 Play the game

- Put five or six children in a circle at the front of the class. Another child stands in the middle.

- The child in the middle chooses someone in the circle. He/She shakes hands with that child and asks *What's your name?* The other child answers then has a turn in the middle.

- To make it a game, play music and let children walk or skip in a circle, or lead the class in clapping a beat. The child in the middle must ask the name of the child standing in front of him/her when the music/clapping stops.

- Children should say *I'm … .* Less able children answer with just their names.

- Set up the game again with a different group of children.

Extension activities

- Let pairs of children come to the front. They practise the question and answer.

- Do the activity in rows or groups. The first child asks the question, the second answers, then asks the third, and so on.

 page 22

1 Write

For detailed guidance notes on handwriting practice, see the teaching notes on page 19 (Workbook, Lesson 1, Activity 1).

- Children write over the arrowed lines in the number 7s, starting at the dot and following the numbered arrows.

- They write over the tinted numbers in the same way, then write independently.

- They do the same with 8.

Lesson 2

Performance indicators

Children will be able to:
- ask someone's age
- give their own age
- write *h* and *H* correctly.

New language

How old are you?
I'm (6).

Review language

What's your name?
I'm ... .

Bring to the lesson

- the Tape
- the Flashcards for Karim and Leila
- age badges

Preparation

- Make age badges for 6 and 7 for the two character Flashcards.
- Make several age badges to use with the class. Make sure there are enough badges with the correct ages on so that each pupil has an appropriate badge (see **Presentation**).

PB **page 23** WB **page 23**

Warm-up

- Greet the class with *Good morning, boys and girls/class.*

- Say to a child *Good morning. I'm ... . What's your name?* Prompt *Good morning, Mr/Mrs/Miss ... . I'm ... .* Do this with a few other children.

- Bring four children to the front of the class. They stand in a line facing the class. Say to child 1 *What's your name?* Prompt, e.g. *I'm Mona*. Child 1 faces child 2 and asks *What's your name?* Child 2 answers then asks child 3, and so on.

- Bring four other children forward. The whole class asks the question. The first child answers. Class repeats the question. The next child answers, and so on.

Presentation

- Show the Flashcard of Karim. Class names him. Stick it on the board. Show the age badge. Prompt *6*. Stick it on the Flashcard. Point and say *Karim, 6*.
- Do the same with Leila and the age card for 7.

- Bring a child forward. Show age badges for 6 and 7. Ask *How old are you?* The child can point or say one of the numbers. Say the sentence, e.g. *I'm 7*. Child repeats. Give him/her the age badge to hold up and show to the class. Repeat the question and elicit the answer once more.

- Do the same with other children.

PB **page 23**

🔘 1 Listen and find

- Children look at the picture in their books for a moment or two. Tell them to listen. They must point to the children when they give their ages.

- Play the first question and answer on the Tape. Stop the Tape. Check that children are pointing to Karim. Continue the Tape. Stop it again, if necessary, to check that they are pointing correctly. You may wish to teach the meaning of the word *only* in the last line.

Tapescript

Narrator: Topic 2. Lesson 2. Activity 1. Listen and find.

Rania: How old are you, Karim?

Karim: I'm 6. [pause]

Rania: And how old are you, Leila?

Leila: I'm 7. [pause] How old are you Rania?

Rania: Oh. I'm only 6. (sigh)

2 Talk

- Bring a child forward. Put age badges for 6 and 7 on your desk. Ask *How old are you?* Prompt the child to hold up an age badge and answer, e.g. *I'm 6.*

- Bring another child forward. Prompt the class to ask the question. The child holds up a badge and answers.

- Do this several times with different children until the class asks confidently.

- Divide the class in two. Prompt one half to ask the question. Choose a child from the other side to hold up an age badge and answer. Do this several times.

- Children ask and answer with a partner. Go round listening to them.

Extension activity

- Bring a child forward and start this dialogue. Play speaker A yourself:

  A: Hello. I'm … . What's your name?
  B: I'm … .
  A: How old are you?
  B: I'm … .

- Demonstrate again, varying the greeting between *Hello* and *Good morning*.

- Let children practise this dialogue in pairs. Child B can also ask *How old are you?* at the end and elicit an answer from child A. Let one or two pairs demonstrate to the class.

 page 23

1 Write

For detailed guidance notes on handwriting practice, see the teaching notes on page 19 (Workbook, Lesson 1, Activity 1).

- Children write over the dotted lines inside the letter *h* next to the exemplar, following the arrows in order.

- They write over the tinted letters *h* starting at the dot.

- They complete the rows starting at the dot.

- They write a row independently, keeping within the guidelines.

- They do the same for the letter *H*.

Lesson 3

Performance indicators

Children will be able to:
- give a simple instruction
- follow a simple instruction
- name four new classroom objects
- write 9 and 10 correctly.

New language

box, chalk, paper, scissors
Bring me the … , please.
(optional) *Thank you.*

Review language

How old are you? I'm … .
What is it? It's a … .
apple, ball, cat, dog, goat, insect
pen, pencil, book, bag, ruler, rubber,
crayon

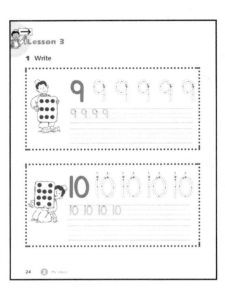

Bring to the lesson

- the Tape
- real classroom objects, e.g. book, pen, pencil, ruler, rubber, etc. Include the new language items (scissors, chalk, paper and box)
- the alphabet exemplar Flashcards for a–i
- the Flashcards 1–10

PB **page 24**   WB **page 24**

Warm-up

- Ask individual children *How old are you?* Elicit *I'm … .* Bring children to the front to ask each other the question and answer.

- Use Flashcards and classroom items to revise words for objects. Show a Flashcard or item (not apple, egg or insect) to the class. Ask *What is it?* Prompt, e.g. *It's a pen.* Do this a few times, changing the object. Also ask individuals.

- Bring three or four children to the front. Give each one a Flashcard. Prompt the class to ask *What is it?* The first child shows the Flashcard and says, e.g. *It's a dog.* The class asks the question again. The next child answers, and so on.

Presentation

- Show the first three new objects (scissors, chalk and paper) one at a time. Say the words. The class repeats.

- Hold up each item keeping the same order. The class says the word.

- Hold up the items in any order. The class says the word.

- Introduce the final word (*box*) and practise.

- Show all four items in any order. The class names them.

PB **page 24**

1 Listen, point and say

- Children look in their books. Tell them to listen for the name of each object. When they hear it, they point to the picture and repeat the word in the pause.

- Play the Tape without stopping. Check to see that children are pointing correctly.

Tapescript

Narrator: Topic 2. Lesson 3. Activity 1. Listen, point and say.

Voice: Scissors. [ping] [pause]

Chalk. [ping] [pause]

Paper. [ping] [pause]

Box. [ping] [pause]

● Play the Tape once more or say the words yourself. Children repeat.

2 Play the game

● Children study the picture. Ask them to name the objects on the table.

● Point out Leila about to pick up the scissors. Ask children to guess what Samir is saying (*Bring me the scissors, please.*).

● Ask the class to suggest what Samir might ask for next. What would he say? Help the class to form several requests like the first.

● Play the *Bring me the … , please game* with the whole class:

1 Put on your desk all 10 objects that are shown on page 24 (box, bag, ball, apple, book, pen, pencil, scissors, paper, chalk).

2 Divide the class into two. A child from Team A asks a child from Team B, e.g. *Bring me the book, please.* The child from Team B finds the correct object. He/She takes it to Team A, who all say *Thank you.*

3 If this is all done correctly, both teams get a point. Then it is Team B's turn to ask. If a child brings the wrong object it must be put back on the desk. The other team wins a point.

Extension activities

● Put Flashcards for the numbers 1 to 10 on the board. Ask children around the class, e.g. *Mona, bring me number 6 please. Thank you*.

● Play the *Bring me the … , please game* using number or picture Flashcards of other objects the children can name.

 page 24

1 Write

For detailed guidance notes on handwriting practice, see the teaching notes on page 19 (Workbook, Lesson 1, Activity 1).

● Children write over the arrowed lines in the number 9s, starting at the dot and following the numbered arrows.

● They write over the tinted numbers in the same way, then write independently.

● They do the same with number 10.

Lesson 4

Performance indicators

Children will be able to:
- recognise and name the letters *j*, *k* and *l*
- match phonic sounds /dʒ/, /k/ and /l/ to written letters *j*, *k* and *l*
- name three new objects
- Write *i* and *l* correctly.

New language

jug, key, lion

Review language

Letters and sounds *a–i*

Bring to the lesson

- the Tape
- the Flashcards for jug, key and lion
- the Flashcards for the letters a–i
- a few real objects or Flashcards for the Warm-up activities

PB **page 25**   WB **page 25**

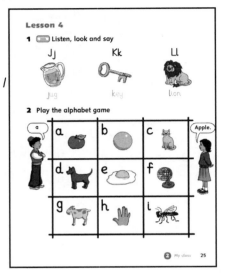

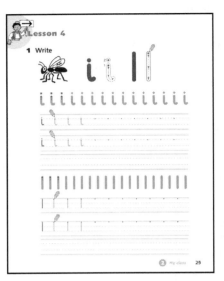

Warm-up

- Play the *Bring me the ... , please game* using real classroom objects and Flashcards.
- Ask individuals *How old are you?* Elicit answers. Let a few children ask the question and elicit answers from other children.

Presentation

- Hold up the alphabet Flashcard for the letter *j*, with the picture showing. Say *jug*. Class repeats. Turn the card to show the letter j. Prompt the class to name it.
- Continue to show *j*. Say *j*, /dʒ/. Turn the card and show the picture. Say *jug*. Do this again and prompt the class to join in saying *j*, /dʒ/, *jug*.
- Do the same with the *k* and *l* Flashcards.

PB **page 25**

🔘🔘 1 Listen, look and say

- Children look in their books at the three pictures for a moment. Tell them to listen and look at the first letter and picture. Play the sequence for *j* on the Tape. Pause the Tape.
- Point to the jug in the book. Prompt the children to point. Check they have the correct picture. Say *j*, /dʒ/, *jug*. Children repeat.
- Follow the procedure in the same way for *k* and *l*.
- Play the Tape without stopping. Children point in their books and repeat.

Tapescript

Narrator: Topic 2. Lesson 4. Activity 1. Listen, look and say.

Voice: j. [pause] /dʒ/. [pause] Jug. [pause]

k. [pause] /k/. [pause] Key. [pause]

l. [pause] /l/. [pause] Lion. [pause]

2 Play the alphabet game

- Go through the letter sounds and exemplar objects, from *a* to *i*, in alphabetical order.

  1 Say /æ/ and hold up the letter *a* Flashcard at the same time.

  2 Children find the letter in their books. They point to the object in the square. Demonstrate using your own book, if necessary.

  3 Turn the Flashcard to show the picture. Class names it: *apple*. Continue with the other letters.

- Use the Pupil's Book and Flashcards to play game A, B or C.

  Game A   Follow steps 1–3 above, but show letters in any order.

  Game B   As game A, but prompt the class to name the object without showing the Flashcard picture.

  Game C   In any order, say a letter sound, but do not show the letter or the picture. Children find the letter in their books and name the object.

Note: If you play this game several times your class should progress from version A, the easiest, to C, the hardest. Less able children can take turns to find and hold up the Flashcard after the class has named the object. Say to these children *Find the … , please. Thank you.*

Extension activities

- Play the *Alphabet game* in teams. Say a letter sound. The first team to name the object starting with that letter wins a point. Then all the children find and point to the object in their books.

- Play the *Alphabet game* in pairs using books. One child points to a letter and says the sound, the other points to the correct picture and names the object.

- Play any version of the alphabet game adding in /dʒ/, jug, /k/, key and /l/, lion.

 page 25

1 Write

For detailed guidance notes on handwriting practice, see the teaching notes on page 19 (Workbook, Lesson 1, Activity 1).

- Children write over the dotted lines inside the letter *i* next to the exemplar, following the arrows in order.

- They write over the tinted letters *i* starting at the dot.

- They complete the rows starting at the dot.

- They write a row independently, keeping within the guidelines.

- They do the same for the letter *l*.

Lesson 5

Performance indicators

Children will be able to:
- name the colours green, yellow and blue
- (optional) follow the instructions *Stand up* and *Sit down*
- write *j* and *J* correctly.

New language

green, yellow, blue

Review language

jug, key, lion

Bring to the lesson

- the Tape
- the Flashcards for green, yellow and blue
- sets of small colour cards for green, yellow and blue

Preparation

Make sets of small colour cards in green, yellow and blue, (see Activity 2, Play the colour game) enough for one card for each child. See page 162 for further details about making teaching resources.

PB **page 26**   WB **page 26**

Warm-up

- Drill the numbers 1 to 10 using any of the number activities your class enjoys.
- Play the *Bring me … , please game* using letters stuck on the board (*Bring me /k/, etc.*) and picture Flashcards or real classroom objects: a pen, a bag, a book, a pencil, etc.

Presentation

- Use the Flashcards to present the three new colours. Hold up the green Flashcard and say *green*. Class repeats. Do this until they say the word confidently.
- Do the same with the yellow and blue Flashcards.

 PB **page 26**

1 Listen, point and say

- Let children look at the colours in their books for a moment. Tell them to listen.

- Play the first part of the Tape. Show the class how to point to each colour as the word is said and repeat it in the pauses. Do this until the class speaks correctly. Stop the Tape.
- Put the colour Flashcards on the board in the same order as in the book. Point to each one. The class says the colours.

Tapescript

Narrator: Topic 2. Lesson 5. Activity 1. Listen, point and say.

Voice: Green. [pause]

Yellow. [pause]

Blue. [pause]

- Play the next part of the Tape. The class points to the colours and says the words.

Tapescript

Narrator: Now listen again, point and say with me.

Voice: Green, yellow, blue.

[pause]

Green, yellow, blue.

[pause]

2 Play the colour game

● Put children in groups of 3 or 4. Give each group a set of 3 or 4 small colour cards. They place them face down.

● Children take turns to turn over a card and show it. The other children take turns to name the colour. The card is put back face down and the three cards mixed up again.

● Less able children have the cards face up and do not change the order. They take turns to point to the colours. Another child in the group says the word.

Extension activity

Note: If you plan to do this activity, and have not already taught *Stand up* and *Sit down*, do so now. Give each instruction a few times for the class to practise the action.

● Give out small colour cards in green, yellow and blue, one per child. Children hold up their cards so that you can see what each child has.

● Call out a colour. All the children holding that colour stand up. Check to see that they have done this correctly.

● Call out the colours several times in any order.

● Children swap cards so that they practise listening out for another colour.

Alternative: Say a child's name. The child must stand up, show his/her colour card and say the word correctly.

 page 26

1 Write

For detailed guidance notes on handwriting practice, see the teaching notes on page 19 (Workbook, Lesson 1, Activity 1).

● Children write over the dotted lines inside the letter *j* next to the exemplar, following the arrows in order.

● They write over the tinted letters *j* starting at the dot.

● They complete the rows starting at the dot.

● They write a row independently, keeping within the guidelines.

● They do the same for the letter *J*.

Lesson 6

Performance indicators

Children will be able to:
- practise naming colours
- practise naming objects
- colour items from dictated instructions
- write *k* and *K* correctly.

New language

game

Review language

green, yellow, blue

Bring to the lesson

- six sets of small picture cards for pencil, pen and book
- the Flashcards for green, yellow and blue
- the number Flashcards

Preparation

- Use Resources page 167 to make six picture cards each of pencils, pens and books. Colour two of the pencils green, two yellow and two blue. Do the same for the pens and the books.
- Make sure children have blue, green and yellow colouring pencils.

PB **page 27**   WB **pages 27 and 28**

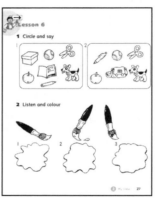

Warm-up

- Revise all classroom objects using real items and Flashcards. Ask *What is it?* Prompt *It's a … .*
- Use number Flashcards to review *What number is it?*

Presentation

- Put the three colour Flashcards on different walls. Say a colour. Children point to that Flashcard and repeat the word.
- Say the colours several times in any order, getting faster.

 PB **page 27**

1 Play the Flashcard game

- Children look at the picture in their books. Point to the whole picture. Say *It's a game*. Bring a child forward.

Say *It's a game* again. Hold up the pre-prepared picture cards for, e.g. a green pen, a yellow book and a blue pencil. Say *blue*. Elicit *pencil*. Show the child how to put the blue pencil under the blue Flashcard.

- Do this again with different children and different picture cards, e.g. a blue book, a yellow pencil, a green pen. Say *green*. Elicit *pen*.

- Divide the class into two teams. Show three more picture cards of different coloured objects to Team A and say a colour. A child names the object which is that colour. He/She places it under the correct Flashcard and wins a point. Do the same with Team B.

- Continue until all the picture cards have been placed under the correct colour Flashcard. If a child makes a mistake, the other team can win a point if they can name the object correctly.

Extension activities

1 Active team game

- Divide the class into three teams. Give the team leaders the green, blue and yellow Flashcards.

- Say *green*. The green team stands up/put hands up. If they do this together and quickly, give them a point. They sit down/put hands down.

- Do the same with the other two colours.

- Say the colours in any order, getting faster and faster. Change over colours.

2 Quiet pairs activity

- Bring a child to the front. Show the picture on page 27. Say *pen*. The child points to one of the pens in the picture and names the colour.

- Repeat with two or three other children and name different objects.

- Children play in pairs. Child 1 names an object, child 2 points and names the colour. After a few turns the children change over tasks. Go around listening.

WB **pages 27 and 28**

1 Circle and say

- Children look at the two pictures. They circle the objects in picture 1 which are not in picture 2 and name them.

> **Answers**
> *box, book, pencil*

2 Listen and colour

- For this exercise children will need yellow, green and blue coloured pens or pencils.

- Tell the class to listen then say these numbers and colours. Pause after each colour for children to colour in: *1 – yellow. 2 – green. 3 – blue.*

- If children do not have green, they could colour blue over yellow to make green.

3 Write

For detailed guidance notes on handwriting practice, see the teaching notes on page 19 (Workbook, Lesson 1, Activity 1).

- Children write over the dotted lines inside the letter *k* next to the exemplar, following the arrows in order.

- They write over the tinted letters *k* starting at the dot.

- They complete the rows starting at the dot.

- They write a row independently, keeping within the guidelines.

- They do the same for the letter *K*.

Lesson 7

Performance indicators

Children will be able to:
- name the colours black, white and red
- recognise and name letters *m, n* and *o*
- match phonic sounds /m/, /n/ and /ɒ/ to written letters *m, n,* and *o*
- name three new objects
- write *l* and *L* correctly.

New language

black, white, red
monkey, nut, orange

Review language

green, blue, yellow
Stand up. Sit down.

Bring to the lesson

- the Tape
- real items or Flashcards
- the Flashcards for black, white, red, green, blue and yellow
- the alphabet Flashcards for monkey, nest and orange
- sets of small colour cards for black, white, red, green, yellow and blue (Extension activity)

Preparation

Make small colour cards for black, white and red. One per child. See page 162 for preparation instructions.

PB **page 28**   WB **page 29**

Warm-up

- Revise letter names, sounds, and alphabet exemplars for *a–l*.

- Make a pile of picture Flashcards or real objects. Say *Find the … , please. Thank you.*

Note: More able children can take turns to give the instruction *Find the … , please.*

Presentation

- Use the Flashcards to present the three new colours. Hold up the red Flashcard. Say *red*. Class repeats. Do this until they say the word confidently.

- Do the same with the black and white Flashcards.

PB **page 28**

 1 Listen, point and say

- Children look at the colours in their books for a moment. Then tell them to listen.

- Play the first part of the Tape. Children point to each colour as the word is said. They repeat it in the pauses. Stop the Tape.

- Put up the colour Flashcards in the same order. Point. Children say them.

Tapescript

Narrator: Topic 2. Lesson 7. Activity 1. Listen, point and say.

Voice: Black. [pause]

Red. [pause]

White. [pause]

- Play the second part of the Tape. Children point in their books and say the words.

Tapescript

Narrator: Now listen again, point and say with me.

Voice: Black, red, white.

[pause]

Black, red, white.

[pause]

- Point to the Flashcards in any order. The children say the colours.

- Add the green, blue and yellow Flashcards and continue pointing in any order.

- Play the *Colours game* with small cards for the new colours in pairs or groups.

Game A (easier) Children put the colour Flashcards face up and keep them in a fixed order. They take turns to point at a Flashcard. Another child says the colour.

Game B The Flashcards are placed face down and mixed up. In turn, children turn one over. Another child says the colour and turns it back. The Flashcards are mixed again.

2 Listen, look and say

- Hold up the alphabet Flashcard for the letter *m*, with the picture showing. Say *monkey*. Class repeats. Turn the card to show the letter m. Class names it.

- Show the letter. Say *m*, /m/. Show the picture. Say *monkey*. Show them again. Class says *m*, /m/, *monkey*.

- Do the same with the *n* and *o* Flashcards.

- Children look in their books at the three pictures. Tell them to look at the first letter and picture and listen. Play the sequence for *m* on the Tape. Pause the Tape.

- Point to the monkey in the book. Prompt children to point. Check they have the correct picture. Say *m*, /m/, *monkey*. Children repeat.

- Follow the procedure in the same way for *n* and *o*.

- Play the Tape without stopping. Children point in their books and repeat.

Tapescript

Narrator: Topic 2. Lesson 7. Activity 2. Listen, look and say.

Voice: m. [pause] /m/. [pause] Monkey. [pause]

n. [pause] /n/. [pause] Nest. [pause]

o. [pause] /ɒ/. [pause] Orange. [pause]

Extension activity

Play the *Colours game* with the whole class.

- Give out colour cards using the six colours the children know. Each child should have one card.

- Say a colour. All the children with that colour stand up.

 page 29

1 Write

For detailed guidance notes on handwriting practice, see the teaching notes on page 19 (Workbook, Lesson 1, Activity 1).

- Children write over the dotted lines inside the letter *l* next to the exemplar, following the arrows in order.

- They write over the tinted letters *l* starting at the dot.

- They complete the rows starting at the dot.

- They write a row independently, keeping within the guidelines.

- They do the same for the letter *L*.

Lesson 8

Performance indicator

Children will be able to:
- describe an object by colour.

New language

It's (white).

Review language

green, blue, yellow, red, black, white

Bring to the lesson

- the Tape
- colour Flashcards for green, blue, yellow, red, black and white
- classroom items in the six colours
- the pairs of small coloured picture cards of pencils, pens and books from Lesson 6 (see Extension activities)
- small coloured picture cards of cats, dogs, bags and lions

Preparation

Use Resources pages 162–167 to make the following picture cards: four cats, four dogs, two bags and two lions. Colour two of the cat picture cards black and two white (or leave them white). Do the same with the dog picture cards. The bag and lion picture cards should be coloured red. These will be used with the coloured picture cards from Lesson 6.

PB **page 29**   WB **page 30**

Warm-up

- Put the colour Flashcards on the board. Use the number Flashcards to number them 1 to 6. Say, e.g. *number 4*. The class looks and answers, e.g. *red*.

- When you have asked about all the numbers, change the positions of the colour Flashcards and play again.

Presentation

- Hold up a colour Flashcard and elicit, e.g. *green*. Hold up a green book. Say *It's green. It's a book.*

- Hold up e.g. a green pencil. Say *It's green* again. Prompt *It's a pencil*.

- Hold up another Flashcard. Prompt the colour, e.g. *black*. Then show the class other black objects. Help the class to say, e.g. *It's black. It's a pen.*

- Point to/hold up classroom objects in the other colours that the children know. Prompt *It's (+ colour). It's a (+ object).*

PB **page 29**

1 Listen and finish the sentences

- Children look at the pictures in their books for a few moments.

- Tell the class to look at you. Hold up your book. Say *It's blue*. See if any of the children can identify the blue object: *It's a bag*. If they cannot, point to the bag, say *It's blue* and prompt *It's a bag*.

- Do this once more with another object.

- Tell children to listen and look at the pictures in their books. Play the Tape. They complete the sentences by naming the objects. Prompt them if necessary.

Tapescript

Narrator: Topic 2. Lesson 8. Activity 1. Listen and finish the sentences.

Rania: It's black.

Leila: It's a … . [pause]

Rania: It's blue.

Leila: It's a … . [pause]

Rania: It's red.

Leila: It's a … . [pause]

- Play the Tape again. Children speak in the pauses as before. Alternatively, make the colour statements yourself. The class replies, e.g. *It's a dog.*

2 Play the game

- Put the class in pairs. One says *It's* and then a colour. The other identifies the object by its colour and replies *It's a … .* Go around listening to them.
- Less able children point to pictures and say *It's red. It's blue.* etc.

Extension activity

- Play this game with the pencil, pen and book picture cards from Lesson 6 and the dog, cat, bag and lion picture cards that you prepared for this lesson. This will give you 15 pairs of coloured picture cards. You will need enough cards for each child to have one. If you have more than 30 children you will need to add extra pairs of coloured cards, e.g. 2 white/black lions, 2 white/black bags. There should only be one pair of cards in each colour.
- Divide the class into two teams. Then divide the pairs of picture cards to make two sets of cards, so that there is one card from each pair in each set. Distribute one set of picture cards to the children in Team A and the other set to the children in Team B.
- Ask a child from Team A to show his/her picture card and describe it, e.g. *It's red. It's a lion.* The child from Team B who has the other one of the pair shows it and says the same.
- Then a child from Team B shows a picture card and describes it. A child from Team A answers.

- Encourage children to listen, look at their cards and answer quickly. If you wish, give points for quick answers.

Note: These cards can also be used for pairs or small groups to play a matching pairs game.

- The cards are placed face down. The first player turns over a card and says, e.g. *It's red. It's a pencil.*
- He/She then turns over another card and says the colour and names the object.
- If they are the same, the player keeps the cards and has another turn. If they are different, the cards are turned face down again in the same place and it is the next player's turn to try to find a matching pair.
- A group of three or four children can play with seven or eight pairs of cards.

 page 30

1 Write

For detailed guidance notes on handwriting practice, see the teaching notes on page 19 (Workbook, Lesson 1, Activity 1).

- Children write over the dotted lines inside the letter *m* next to the exemplar, following the arrows in order.
- They write over the tinted letters *m* starting at the dot.
- They complete the rows starting at the dot.
- They write a row independently, keeping within the guidelines.
- They do the same for the letter *M*.

Lesson 9

Performance indicators

Children will be able to:
- specify an object by colour
- act out a story.

New language

Bring me the (red box), please.

Review language

green, blue, yellow, red, black, white

Bring to the lesson

- the Tape
- the alphabet Flashcards a–o
- the small letter cards for a–o from Section 2 of the Welcome topic
- three coloured boxes (one red, one blue and one yellow) for Presentation and Activity 2, Act it out.

Preparation

Find or make three coloured boxes (without lids): red, blue and yellow.

PB		WB	
page 30		**page 31**	

Warm-up

- Play the *Object/letter matching game*. Stick the alphabet Flashcards for letters *a* to *o* on the board, with pictures facing the class. Place the small letter cards *a* to *o* face down on your desk.
- Children take turns to turn over a letter card, say the sound and place it beside the correct picture on the board.

Presentation

- Use the coloured boxes you made to teach *It's a (colour word) box*. Show the red box and ask *What is it?* Elicit *It's a box. It's red.* Say *It's a red box.* Class repeats. Do the same with the blue and yellow boxes.

page 30

1 Listen and read

- Children look at the pictures and try to work out the story. Ask for their ideas.

- Tell them to listen and follow in their books. Play the Tape.

Tapescript

Narrator: Topic 2. Lesson 9. Activity 1. Listen and read.

Salama: Bring me the red box, please. [pause]

Bring me the blue box, please. [pause]

And the yellow box, please. [pause]

Find the chalk.

Boy: Wow!

- Ask children who they think is helping Salama (his brother).
- Hold up your book, point to each picture and read out the speech bubble. Children repeat after you.
- Ask them how they think the chalk got under the yellow box. Listen to some of their suggestions, then play the Tape again if you wish.

2 Act it out

- Divide children into groups. Three children play Salama, his brother and the child looking for the chalk. The others are the audience. Groups practise, then take turns to perform to the rest of the class using the boxes you made.

Note:

- The child who is Salama hides chalks up his/her sleeve. He/She distracts the audience when his brother fetches the last box and removes the chalk from the red box. When the child is looking under the red box Salama quickly puts all the chalk under the yellow box.

- For more speaking practice, let four children each say one of Salama's instructions.

- Variation: Children can vary this by hiding other objects under the box, e.g. rubbers, pens, crayons.

Extension activity

- Play the *Please instruction game*. Tell the class you will give them an instruction. If you say *please* at the end they must do it. If you do not, they must do nothing. If they move, they are out.

- Put the three coloured boxes around the classroom. You can also put real items or Flashcards for vocabulary that you would like to practise around the classroom.

- Give instructions to the whole class, e.g *Point to the red box, please. Stand up, please. Sit down, please. Point to a pen*. Any child who points to the pen is out.

- Give instructions until you have a winner. Alternatively, play with the class in two teams. Count which team has the most players left when you decide to finish the game.

WB page 31

1 Listen, say and colour

- Point to the first circle. Say *red*. Children repeat and colour.

- Continue with the other two circles. (Circle 2: white – children leave it blank. Circle 3: black.)

2 Colour and say

- Children colour the pictures in red, black, white (leave blank), green, blue or yellow. They choose which colours to use for each object. They can use the same colour more than once if they wish.

- In pairs they practise asking *What is it?* Children answer, e.g. *It's a lion. It's yellow*. More able pupils should be encouraged to answer with the colour word and the noun, e.g. *It's a yellow lion*. Listen to pairs.

Note: This structure is presented and practised more extensively in Topic 3, Lesson 1.

Lesson 10

Performance indicators

Children will be able to:
- sing a song
- recognise and name the letters *p*, *q* and *r*
- match the phonic sounds /p/, /q/ and /r/ to the letters *p*, *q* and *r*
- name two new objects
- write *n* and *N* correctly.

New language

queen, ring
stop, go, clean, bright, new, very

Review language

green, blue, yellow, red, black, white, pen

Bring to the lesson

- the Tape
- pairs of real socks or paper/card socks in all the colours (see Presentation).
- paper socks for children to colour (see Activity 1, Sing)
- 2 large cards, one with a red circle and one with a green circle
- the alphabet Flashcards for p, q and r

Preparation

- Take two pieces of paper or card. On one of them draw and colour a large red circle. On the other draw and colour a large green circle (see Warm-up).
- If you don't have the real socks, use Resources page 168 to make 6 pairs of paper socks, one in each of the 6 colours.
- Use Resources pages 168 to make one paper sock for each child (for the song).

PB page 31   **WB** page 32

Warm-up

- Play the *Stop and go game* with the two circles. Show the red circle. Prompt *It's red*.

- Walk on the spot. Hold up the red circle. Say *Stop* and stand still.

- Show the green circle. Prompt *It's green*. Say *Go* and walk on the spot.

- Class stands up. Show the green circle. Say *Go*. Children walk on the spot. Show the red circle. Say *Stop*. Children stand still. Do this a few times until the class is confident that red means stop and green means go.

- Play a game in two teams. Show one team the circles one at a time. They say *Stop* or *Go*. The other team stands still or walks on the spot. Change over after a few turns.

Presentation

- Show children at least one real pair of socks. Say *socks* and hold them up. Children repeat. (Plural nouns are fully introduced in Topic 3, Lesson 8.)

- Show real or paper socks in all the colours in the song. Say, e.g. *red socks*. Children repeat. Stick them on the board. Do the same with the other pairs.

- Use real socks to explain *clean*, *bright* and *new*, or

translate these words. Also, teach the meaning of the word *very*.

page 31

 1 Sing

● Say the words of the song and point to the correct colour socks on the board as you speak. Children point to the socks in their books.

● Play the Tape. Children listen and point again.

Tapescript

Narrator: Topic 2. Lesson 10. Activity 1. Sing.

Children: Red socks,

Green socks,

Very, very clean socks.

Black socks,

White socks,

Very, very bright socks.

Yellow socks,

Blue socks,

Very, very new socks.

● Give out one of the paper socks you have prepared to each child. Children colour them. Tell them which colour to use. There should be a roughly equal number of socks in each colour (green, yellow, blue, red, black, white).

● Bring a child to the front with his/her sock. Class names the colour. Bring up a child with a different colour. Class names the first colour and adds the new colour. Continue to add new children and colours. The class names the colours from the beginning each time.

● Sing the song again with all the children holding up the correct colour socks as they are named. Encourage them to join in with the song.

 2 Listen, look and say

● Hold up the alphabet Flashcard for the letter *p*, with the picture showing. Say *pen*. Class repeats. Turn the card to show the letter *p*. Class names it.

● Show the letter and say *p*, /p/. Show the picture. Say

pen. Show them again. Class says *p*, /p/, *pen*.

● Do the same with the *q* and *r* Flashcards.

● Children look in their books at the three pictures. Tell them to look at the first letter and picture and listen. Play the sequence for *p* on the Tape. Pause the Tape.

● Point to the pen in the book. Prompt children to point. Check they have the correct picture. Say *p*, /p/, *pen*. Children repeat.

● Follow the procedure in the same way for *q* and *r*.

● Play the Tape without stopping. Children point in their books and repeat.

Tapescript

Narrator: Topic 2. Lesson 10. Activity 2. Listen, look and say.

Voice: p. [pause] /p/. [pause] Pen. [pause]

q. [pause] /q/. [pause] Queen. [pause]

r. [pause] /r/. [pause] Ring. [pause]

Extension activity

● Six children with different coloured socks stand in a line in any order. Children hold up their socks one by one. Class names the colour.

● Change the order of children in the line. Do the activity again.

● Repeat with another six children.

 page 32

1 Write

For detailed guidance notes on handwriting practice, see the teaching notes on page 19 (Workbook, Lesson 1, Activity 1).

● Children write over the dotted lines inside the letter *n* next to the exemplar, following the arrows in order.

● They write over the tinted letters *n* starting at the dot.

● They complete the rows starting at the dot.

● They write a row independently, keeping within the guidelines.

● They do the same for the letter *N*.

Lesson 11 – Review

Performance indicators

Children will be able to:
- use and understand the language taught in Lessons 1–10
- write *o* and *O* correctly
- write *p* and *P* correctly.

New language

picture

Review

greetings and introductions
What is it?
It's (green).
It's a ... .
1, 2, 3, 4, 5, 6, 7, 8, 9, 10

Bring to the lesson

- the Tape
- the Flashcards for numbers and colours (green, yellow, blue, red, black, white)
- the alphabet Flashcards for a–r

 page 32   WB **pages 33 and 34**

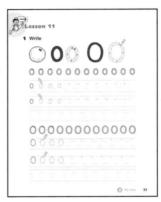

Warm-up

- Sing *Hello and good morning* from Topic 1, Lesson 10. One side of the class sings to the other.

- Say to individual children *Hello. What's your name?* Children respond. Ask *How old are you?* Children respond.

- Bring children forward to introduce themselves to the class, e.g. *Hello. I'm Ali. I'm 6.* etc.

Presentation

- Hold up your book. Point to the first picture. Say *picture*. Prompt the class to repeat a few times.

- Point out the numbers 1 and 2. Point to the first picture and say *picture 1*. Class repeats. Do the same with picture 2.

PB **page 32**

1 Listen and answer

- Check vocabulary. Hold up your book. Say, e.g. *Look at picture 1*. Point to an object in the picture. Ask *What is it?* Elicit *It's a ... .* Repeat with all the objects in the pictures.

- Tell children to look in their books and listen. Play the Tape. Children answer the questions in the pauses.

Tapescript

Narrator: Topic 2. Lesson 11. Activity 1. Listen and answer.

Voice: Look at picture 1.

It's red. What is it? [pause]

Look at picture 2.

It's blue. What is it? [pause]

Look at picture 1 again.

It's blue. What is it? [pause]

Now look at picture 2.

It's yellow. What is it? [pause]

Answers
ball (red, picture 1*)*, *book* (blue, picture 2), *fan*
(blue, picture 1), *dog* (yellow, picture 2)

2 Play the game

● Demonstrate how the game works. Make a statement
about an object, e.g. *It's a fan. It's white.* Prompt the
answer *Picture 2*.

● Children can do this activity in pairs. Alternatively, go
through all the items with the whole class. This can be
as a single group or in teams taking turns.

Extension activities

● Use Flashcards and objects to revise structures and
vocabulary taught in this topic.

● Choose any of the games that the children have
enjoyed (see page 9).

 pages 33 and 34

1 Write

For detailed guidance notes on handwriting practice, see
the teaching notes on page 19 (Workbook, Lesson 1,
Activity 1).

● Children write over the dotted lines inside the letter *o*
next to the exemplar, following the arrows in order.

● They write over the tinted letters *o* starting at the dot.

● They complete the rows starting at the dot.

● They write a row independently, keeping within the
guidelines.

● They do the same for the letter *O*.

2 Write

● Children practise writing *p* and *P* as in Activity 1,
above.

Lesson 12

Performance indicators

Children will be able to:
- practise naming the six colours
- consolidate descriptive language.

Review language

green, yellow, blue, red, black, white
It's ... .
It's a ... .

Bring to the lesson

- the red and green circles (from Lesson 10)
- the Flashcards for colours (blue, green, yellow, red, black, white)
- real classroom objects in the six colours
- small colour cards (from Lessons 5 and 7)
- two uncoloured picture cards of objects children have learned for each child in the class

Preparation

Use Resources pages 162–167 to make enough picture cards of objects the children have learned for all of them in the class to have two each.

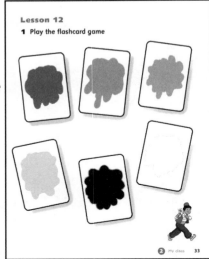

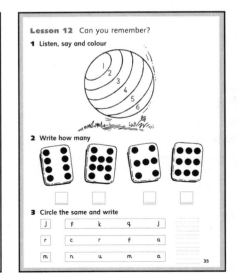

PB **page 33**   WB **page 35**

Warm-up

- Sing the song from Lesson 10.
- Play the *Stop and go game* (Warm-up, Lesson 10) in four or five numbered teams.

  1 Give the leader of each team a number Flashcard to hold up.

  2 Hold up the red or green circle and instruct each team to go or stop, e.g. *1, go. 4, go. 1, stop. 2, go,* etc. Teams walk on the spot or stand completely still.

  3 More than one team can be moving at a time. Start the game slowly. When children are used to the instructions say them faster. Children have to concentrate and listen out for their number.

  4 After a few turns, change over numbers.

Presentation

- Bring six children forward. They stand in a line. Give each one a colour Flashcard.

- Starting from the right, they hold up their Flashcards in turn. Class says the colour. Immediately, the child holding that Flashcard runs to the other end of the line. The other children move up so the next colour can be named at once.

- Encourage the children holding the Flashcards to move quickly, and the class to name colours quickly, so that the class says the words together in a chant.

- When the class has got used to this activity, tell the children with Flashcards to hold them face down and change places. Continue with the new positions.

PB **page 33**

1 Play the Flashcard game

- Bring six children forward to stand in a line and hold a

colour Flashcard each, face down. Tell the class to look at page 33 in their books. Call out the name of a child with a Flashcard. The child holds it up. Other children point to the same colour Flashcard in their books and name the colour.

● With all the children sitting down in their places, hold up objects in different colours. Say *It's a pencil.* Class replies *It's blue* (or *It's a blue pencil* if children have already taken in this structure). They point to the correct colour in their books.

Extension activities

Game with the whole class

● Bring six more children to stand in a line at the front and hold colour Flashcards.

● Give out small colour cards to the rest of the class. All children show colours.

● Say the name of a child holding a colour Flashcard. The child holds up his/her Flashcard and says the colour. All the children with that colour stand up and name it. Check that they are correct and continue.

Pairs activity

● Give each child any two coloured pictures from Resources pages 162–167. They colour them as they choose.

● In pairs, children show their partners one of their pictures and say the colour. The partner says what it is. Any pairs who are more advanced say, e.g. *It's a blue bag.*

● Children change cards with another pair and talk about their pictures.

WB **page 35**

● This page can be used as a test to check class progress in work covered in Topic 2. Give children a fixed length of time to complete each activity.

● Prepare examples of exercises 2 and 3 and do them on the board so that children know what to do in their books.

● Alternatively, use this page as normal Workbook exercises and explain each task in turn, keeping the whole class working together.

1 Listen, say and colour

● Tell children to listen. Say these numbers and colours: *1 – red; 2 – black, 3 – green, 4 – yellow, 5 – blue, 6 – white.* (Alternatively, hold up the number Flashcard as you say each colour.) Give children time to colour.

2 Write how many

● Children count the number of dots on each card and write the numbers in the boxes underneath.

Answers
8, 10, 7, 9

3 Circle the same and write

● Children look at each line of letters and identify the two that are the same. They circle them and write the letter in the grid on the right.

3 My colours

In this topic pupils:

- name twelve new objects (Lessons 1, 3, 4, 7 and 10)
- name the new colours pink, purple, orange, brown, grey (Lesson 7)
- describe objects by colour (Lesson 1)
- learn four new classroom instructions
- ask about colour and describe a two-coloured object (Lesson 2)
- follow and act out stories (Lesson 9)
- recognise and say the sounds for letters *s–z* (Lessons 4, 7 and 10)
- ask and answer about the colour of objects (Lesson 5)
- ask about numbers of items (Lesson 8)
- sing a song (Lesson 10)
- practise and consolidate (Lessons 3, 6, 9, 11 and 12)
- write the letters *qQ–zZ* correctly (Lessons 1, 2, 4, 5, 6, 7, 8, 10 and 11).

Lesson 1

Performance indicators

Children will be able to:
- name four new objects
- describe objects by colour
- write *q* and *Q* correctly.

New language

plane, tree, balloon, bird
It's a (yellow) (plane).

Review language

colours
stop, go

Bring to the lesson

- the Tape
- the Flashcards for plane, tree, balloon and bird
- the Flashcards for colours (yellow, green, blue, red, black, white)

| PB | **page 34** | | WB | **page 36** |

Warm-up

- Divide the class into six teams. Give a colour Flashcard to each team.

- Play the *Stop and go game*. Teams walk on the spot or stand still according to your instructions, e.g. *Blue, go. White, go. Blue, stop. Green, go*, etc.

- Play a few times, then teams swap colours.

Presentation

- Show the class the plane Flashcard. Point and say *plane*. Class repeats. Do this until they speak confidently.
- Show the Flashcard of one of the other objects and name it, e.g. *balloon*. Class repeats. Do this until they speak confidently.
- Introduce the third object in the same way.
- Hold up the three Flashcards in random order. Children say the words.
- Introduce the last object then revise all four.
- Show the tree. Ask *What is it?* Elicit *It's a tree*. Say *Yes. It's a green tree*.
- Continue in the same way with the other three new words.
- Show the tree. Ask *What is it?* Prompt the class to reply *It's a green tree*. Do the same with the other pictures.

 page 34

 1 Listen and find

- Tell the class to listen and look in their books.
- Start the Tape. Stop it after Samir speaks the first time. Say *Point to the green tree*. Check children are pointing correctly.
- Play the rest of the Tape. Check children are pointing correctly.
- If you wish, play the Tape again straight through.

Tapescript

Narrator: Topic 3. My colours. Lesson 1. Activity 1. Listen and find.

Rania: Find the tree. It's green.

Samir: Yes. A green tree. [giggle]

Rania: Yes. Good. Now find the plane. It's yellow.

Samir: Hmm! A yellow plane. Oh, look!

Rania: And now find the balloon. It's red.

Samir: Oh, yes. It's a red balloon.

Rania: Find the bird. It's white.

Samir: Here it is. A white bird.

Rania: Well done, Samir!

---

2 Point and say

- In pairs children take turns to point in their books and ask *What is it?* and reply, e.g. *It's a yellow plane*.
- Make sure children also ask about the dog and the bag, not mentioned on the Tape.

Extension activity

- Choose real items and Flashcards of objects, each in one of the colours children can name.
- Divide the class into two teams. Show Team A an object/Flashcard. Ask *What is it?* If they answer correctly they get a point. If they cannot, it is Team B's turn to answer. Children should give complete answers, e.g. *It's a black pen*.
- Play a few times then prompt teams to take turns to join in asking the question.

 page 36

1 Write

For detailed guidance notes on handwriting practice, see the teaching notes on page 19 (Workbook, Lesson 1, Activity 1).

- Children write over the dotted lines inside the letter *q* next to the exemplar, following the arrows in order.
- They write over the tinted letters *q* starting at the dot.
- They complete the rows starting at the dot.
- They write a row independently, keeping within the guidelines.
- They do the same for the letter *Q*.

Lesson 2

Performance indicators

Children will be able to:
- ask about the colour of something
- describe a two-coloured object.
- write r and R correctly.

New language

What colour is the ... ?

Review language

colours

Bring to the lesson

- the Tape
- a tray or a box with a cloth to cover it
- real items in one or two colours (see Activity 2, Play the game)

Preparation

Find three or more large objects, e.g. a bag, an umbrella and a ball, in two colours children know. (Alternatively, draw balloon shapes and colour them in two colours.)

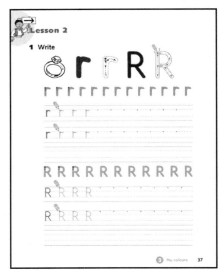

PB **page 35**   WB **page 37**

Warm-up

- Hold up some items in one colour that children can name. Prompt, e.g. *It's a red book.*

Presentation

- Show one of your two-coloured objects. Say, e.g. *It's red and yellow.* Point to the two different colours as you speak. Repeat with another object.

- Show a third object. Point to the two colours and prompt the class to say, e.g. *It's blue and green.*

- Hold up any picture of an object or real object in a single colour that children know. Ask, e.g. *What colour is the book?* Elicit, e.g. *It's green.* Do this with a few more items.

- Ask the same question about some two-coloured objects and elicit, e.g. *It's black and white.*

 PB **page 35**

1 Listen and point

- Let children look at the picture for a few moments. Tell them to listen and point to the objects they hear on the Tape.

- Play the Tape. Check that children are pointing to the correct object. Stop the Tape if necessary, for children to find it. They repeat the answers in the pauses.

Tapescript

Narrator: Topic 3. Lesson 2. Activity 1. Listen and point.

Voice: What colour is the insect? [pause] It's black. [pause]

What colour is the bird? [pause] It's yellow. [pause]

What colour is the balloon? [pause] It's red and white. [pause]

What colour is the ball? [pause] It's yellow and white. [pause]

What colour is the apple? [pause] It's red. [pause]

- Play the Tape a second time without stopping if you wish.

2 Play the game

- Place three or four items of one or two colours on a tray or in a shallow box.

- Hold up each item in turn. Ask *What colour is the ... ?* Children answer.

- If you have some more able children, let them take turns to ask the question as you hold up the object.

- Cover the items with a cloth. Ask, e.g. *What colour is the ball?* Children try to remember.

- Start with only three or four items and add more if the children are good at remembering the objects and colours.

- When the class has answered questions a few times, let individuals ask questions. The rest of the class answers.

Extension activity

- Children look at the objects on Rania's tray in Activity 2 for a minute or two. Say *Close your books*. Ask, e.g. *What colour is the ... ?* about the objects.

- Children can also ask and answer in pairs using the picture in Activity 1 on this page, and on page 34.

 page 37

1 Write

For detailed guidance notes on handwriting practice, see the teaching notes on page 19 (Workbook, Lesson 1, Activity 1).

- Children write over the dotted lines inside the letter *r* next to the exemplar, following the arrows in order.

- They write over the tinted letters *r* starting at the dot.

- They complete the rows starting at the dot.

- They write a row independently, keeping within the guidelines.

- They do the same for the letter *R*.

Lesson 3

Performance indicators

Children will be able to:
- follow four new classroom instructions
- follow simple hygiene instructions.

New language

Wash your hands.
Dry your hands.
Wipe the table.
Clean the board.

Review language

Instructions with *please*.

Bring to the lesson

- the Tape
- a bowl, a towel and a cloth for wiping the table
- a classroom board rubber and chalk (if not already in the classroom)

 PB **page 36**   **WB** **page 38**

Warm-up

- Sing *Red socks, Green socks* (Topic 2, Lesson 10).

- Write some matching pairs of capital and small letters on the board in random order. Children come to the board and draw lines matching the capitals to the correct small letters. Do not clean the board.

Presentation

- Put the bowl and towel on your desk. Put some chalk marks on your desk. Make sure the children see you do this.

- Bring a child forward. Hold out the board rubber. Say, e.g. *Karim, clean the board, please*.

- Bring a different child forward. Point to the chalk on your desk and say, e.g. *Dina, wipe the table, please*.

- Bring a third child forward. Look at his/her hands and pretend they are dirty. Point to the bowl and say it has water in it. Say *Wash your hands, please*. Prompt the child to mime washing his/her hands. Hold out the towel and say to the same child *Dry your hands, please*. They mime drying their hands.

- Practise the four new instructions with different children until the class is confident.

 **PB** **page 36**

1 Listen, point and say

- Children look at the pictures in their books for a few moments. Tell them to look, listen and point to the correct picture in the pauses. Play the Tape.

Tapescript

Narrator: Topic 3. Lesson 3. Activity 1. Listen, point and say.

Leila: Clean the board. [sound of blackboard being wiped with duster]

[pause]

Karim: Wipe the table. [sound of wet cloth being wiped over table]

	[pause]
Samir:	Wash your hands. [sound of tap running, water splashing, hand washing]
	[pause]
Rania:	Dry your hands. [sound of hands being dried on a towel]
	[pause]

- Hold up your book, point to each picture and say the instruction. Class repeats.
- Play the Tape again. Children listen, point and repeat the instructions in the pause.

2 Guess the actions

- Children look at the picture in their books. Ask if they can say what is happening. (Leila is pretending to do one of the actions. Karim is trying to think what it is.)
- Point out the picture in Karim's thought bubble. Ask if he has guessed correctly.
- Bring a child forward and start the game in the same way. Whisper the instruction to the child, who mimes the action. The class guesses, e.g. *Dry your hands.* Do this a few times with different children.

Extension activities

- Play the *Please instruction game*. Give instructions for actions. Children only do the actions if you say *please*. Include actions from this lesson. Children mime them. Add, e.g. *Stand up. Sit down. Go. Stop.*
- Play the guessing game in Activity 2 with other instructions that can be mimed, e.g. *Open/Close your book*, etc.

 page 38

1 Join the dots and say

- Children join the dots in alphabetical order to complete the picture. They can then colour it and name it, e.g. *It's a red lion*.

2 Join and say

- Children look at the top row of pictures and join them to the matching item in the row below.

Lesson 4

Performance indicators

Children will be able to:

- recognise and say the sounds of the letters *s*, *t* and *u*
- match the phonic sounds /s/, /t/ and /ʌ/ to the written letters *s*, *t* and *u*
- recognise and name three new objects
- write *s* and *S* correctly.

New language

sun, tap, umbrella

Review language

Wash your hands, please.
Dry your hands, please.
Clean the board, please.
Wipe the table, please.

Bring to the lesson

- the Tape
- any four object Flashcards (see Warm-up)

PB **page 37**   WB **page 39**

Warm-up

Play an *Action game* with the whole class.

- Stick four Flashcards of objects in colours the children know on the four walls of the class. Ask *What is it?* and *What colour is it?* as you do so.

- Use all the instructions the children know, e.g. *Stand up. Sit down. Stop. Go. Point to the plane/tree/cat. Wash your hands. Dry your hands. Wipe the table. Clean the board.*

- Give the class the different instructions in any order. Encourage them to do the actions quickly and all together.

Presentation

- Hold up the alphabet Flashcard for the letter *s*, with the picture showing. Say *sun*. Class repeats. Turn the card to show the letter *s*. Class names it.

- Show the letter and say *s*, /s/. Show the picture. Say *sun*. Show them again. Class says *s*, /s/, *sun*.

- Do the same with the *t* and *u* Flashcards.

PB **page 37**

🔘 1 Listen, look and say

- Children look in their books at the three pictures. Tell them to listen and look at the first letter and picture. Play the sequence for *s* on the Tape. Pause the Tape.

- Point to the sun in the book. Prompt children to point. Check they are pointing to the same picture. Say *s*, /s/, *sun* again, pausing for the children to repeat as on the Tape.

- Follow the procedure in the same way for *t* and *u*.

- Play the Tape without stopping. Children point in their books and repeat.

Tapescript

Narrator: Topic 3. Lesson 4. Activity 1. Listen, look and say.

Voice: s. [pause] /s/. [[pause] Sun. [pause]

t. [pause] /t/. [pause] Tap. [pause]

u. [pause] /ʌ/. [pause] Umbrella. [pause]

2 Play the picture game

● Children look at the pictures for a few moments. Say, e.g. *Number 9. What is it?* Elicit *It's a white plane.* If the answer is correct, say *Yes, it's a white plane.* Ask the whole class. They repeat *It's a white plane.* If the answer is wrong, ask another child until you get the correct answer. Continue with the other numbers.

● Tell children to use their pencils. Hold up your book. Say e.g. *The green tree.* Demonstrate circling the picture in the book.

● Name three or four objects in the grid. Give children time to find and circle each one. Check answers. Check understanding by asking, e.g. *The green tree. What number is it?* Elicit *It's number 7.*

● Children take turns to ask and answer in pairs with the book open. Child 1 asks, e.g. *Number 8. What is it?* Child 2 names the object. Children who find asking the question hard can just say the number.

Extension activity

Play a game in two teams using the pictures in Activity 2.

● Give children one minute to look at the pictures. They then shut their books.

● Ask each team in turn, e.g. *Number 4. What is it?* If they answer correctly, they get a point. If they are wrong, the other team may answer and win a point.

 page 39

1 Write

For detailed guidance notes on handwriting practice, see the teaching notes on page 19 (Workbook, Lesson 1, Activity 1).

● Children write over the dotted lines inside the letter *s* next to the exemplar, following the arrows in order.

● They write over the tinted letters *s* starting at the dot.

● They complete the rows starting at the dot.

● They write a row independently, keeping within the guidelines.

● They do the same for the letter *S*.

Lesson 5

Performance indicator

Children will be able to:
● ask and answer questions about the colours of objects
● write *t* and *T* correctly.

New language

What colour is it?

Review

1, 2, 3, 4, 5, 6, 7, 8, 9, 10

Bring to the lesson

● real objects in the six colours
● the Tape
● the Flashcards for objects
● the Flashcards for numbers

 page 38   **page 40**

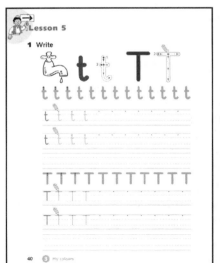

Warm-up

Play the *Number order action game* with the class using Flashcards.

● Five children at the front of the class hold the number Flashcards 1 to 5 in any order.

● Class counts from 1 to 5. The children with Flashcards get into the correct order before the class reaches 5.

● Repeat with the Flashcards for the numbers 6 to 10.

Presentation

● Hold up, e.g. a yellow book. Ask *What is it?* Prompt *It's a book*. Ask *What colour is it?* Prompt *It's yellow*. Do this again with another object and let children answer the question themselves, if they can. Otherwise, prompt them.

● Practise the question and answer until the class can reply confidently. If they find this easy, ask about an object with more than one colour.

 page 38

🔊 1 Listen, find and answer

● Children look at the picture in their books. Say *Find number 3*. Check they are pointing to the correct number. Ask *What colour is it?* Elicit *It's green*.

● Repeat a few times with different numbers.

● Play the first section of the Tape. Prompt children to point to the balloons in the pauses.

Tapescript

Narrator: Topic 3. Lesson 5. Activity 1. Listen, find and answer.

Salama: Find number 4. What colour is it?

Karim: It's red. [pause]

Salama: Find number 7. What colour is it?

Karim: It's green. [pause]

● Play the rest of the Tape. Children answer in the pauses.

Tapescript

Narrator: Now listen, find and answer.

Salama: Find number 2. What colour is it? [pause]

Karim: It's yellow.

Salama: Find number 10. What colour is it? [pause]

Karim: It's white.

Salama: Find number 1. What colour is it? [pause]

Karim: It's blue.

Narrator: Now you try.

- Play the whole Tape again without stopping. Children answer in the pauses.

- Children point in their books and ask and answer in pairs. Listen to some pairs of varying ability to check progress and understanding.

2 Talk

- Bring three more able children to the front. Choose four or five Flashcards of objects in colours that children can name, e.g. *tree, sun, pen, plane,* etc.

- Hold up three so that all the class can see. Say to the first child *Find the pen. What colour is it?* Child answers.

- Change one or two of the Flashcards. Ask the second child to find a different object.

- Change Flashcards again. Show a new Flashcard to the first child. Prompt him/her to say to the second child. *Find the ... . What colour is it?* The second child answers.

- Repeat this with the second and third child.

- Children use the picture in their books to ask and answer in pairs. Alternatively, elicit the questions and answers from individuals around the class.

Extension activity

- Divide the class into two teams. Show a Flashcard just to Team A, e.g. the plane. Team A instructs Team B *Find the plane. What colour is it?*

- Put the plane Flashcard with two or three others then show them to Team B. They look for the plane and say, e.g. *It's red and white.*

- Teams get a point for each task correctly completed. Change the Flashcards after a few turns.

 page 40

1 Write

For detailed guidance notes on handwriting practice, see the teaching notes on page 19 (Workbook, Lesson 1, Activity 1).

- Children write over the dotted lines inside the letter *t* next to the exemplar, following the arrows in order.

- They write over the tinted letters *t* starting at the dot.

- They complete the rows starting at the dot.

- They write a row independently, keeping within the guidelines.

- They do the same for the letter *T*.

Lesson 6

Performance indicators

Children will be able to:
- recognise letters and correctly pronounce the sounds
- name objects with known initial letters
- write *u* and *U* correctly.

Review language

Letters and exemplars *a–u*

Bring to the lesson

- the alphabet Flashcards for *a–u*

 PB **page 39**   **WB** **pages 41 and 42**

Warm-up

- Play the *Action game* (see Warm-up, Lesson 4). Put four or more different Flashcards around the classroom for children to point to during the game.

Presentation

- Use the alphabet Flashcards for the letters which are not on the page: *a, c, d, e, h, i, o, q, s, t* and *u*. Write six of these letters on the board.
- Give out the alphabet Flashcards for those letters to six children. They stand at the front.
- Point to a letter on the board. Class says the sound.
- Prompt the class to name the Flashcard exemplar beginning with that sound. The child holding that Flashcard puts it under the correct letter on the board.
- Repeat with the remaining five letters and Flashcards.
- Occasionally, point to the Flashcard first. The class names the object and the Flashcard is placed under the correct letter.

 PB **page 39**

1 Play the Flashcard game

- Children study the page for a minute or two.
- Point to an object on the page and prompt a child to name it. The class must sound the initial letter.
- Children then find the letter on the page and join it to the object. If possible, tell children to use a different colour for each letter.
- Occasionally, give the letter sound first. Class names the object that begins with that sound and join them with a line.
- Continue like this until all the letters and objects are matched.

Extension activity

Flashcard/letter matching game

Version 1

- Place alphabet Flashcards on your desk and write the matching letters on the board.

- Show the class a Flashcard picture. Ask *What is it?* Class names it, e.g. *Hand*.

- Ask *What letter?* Prompt *h, /h/*. Ask different children to place the Flashcard under the correct letter on the board.

Version 2 (if you have space in your classroom)

- Place all the Flashcards on your desk face up. Write the letters on the board.

- Children take turns to come to your desk, hold up a Flashcard and name the item. Class repeats. Children place the Flashcard under the correct letter then go back and sit down.

- Continue until all the Flashcards are placed.

Note: This can be played as a game for two teams. Change the Flashcards and put them in two piles on your desk. Teams take turns to hold up a Flashcard, name the object, say the letter and position it correctly on the board. The first team to place all their Flashcards correctly wins.

 pages 41 and 42

1 Colour and say

- Children colour the items as they please. Encourage more able children to use two colours.

- In pairs they point in each other's books and say, e.g. *It's blue and green*. More able children can say *It's a blue and green bird*.

2 Write the numbers

- Children complete the sequence of numbers. Check their work and ask individuals to say the numbers as you go round.

- To extend this, they can colour the balloons and play in pairs, e.g. *Find number 6. What colour is it? It's red*.

3 Write

For detailed guidance notes on handwriting practice, see the teaching notes on page 19 (Workbook, Lesson 1, Activity 1).

- Children write over the dotted lines inside the letter *u* next to the exemplar, following the arrows in order.

- They write over the tinted letters *u* starting at the dot.

- They complete the rows starting at the dot.

- They write a row independently, keeping within the guidelines.

- They do the same for the letter *U*.

Lesson 7

Performance indicators

Children will be able to:
- name the colours pink, purple, orange, brown and grey
- recognise and say the sound of the letters *v, w* and *x*
- match the phonic sounds /v/, /w/ and /ks/ to the written letters *v, w* and *x*
- name two new objects
- write *v* and *V* correctly.

New language

pink, purple, orange, brown, grey, van, watch

Review language

colours

Bring to the lesson

- the Tape
- the Flashcards for pink, purple, orange, brown and grey
- the alphabet flashcards for v, w and x
- (optional) sets of small colour cards in the new colours, one for each child (see Extension activities).

Preparation

Make a set of colour cards for the new colours (pink, purple, orange, brown, grey). See page 162 for preparation instructions.

PB **page 40**   WB **page 43**

Warm-up

- Sing *Red socks, Green socks* from Topic 2, Lesson 10.

Presentation

- Use the Flashcards to present the five new colours. Hold up the pink Flashcard and say *pink*. Class repeats. Do this until they say the word confidently.
- Do the same with the other four colours.
- Show the Flashcards in any order. Children name the colours.

PB **page 40**

1 Listen, point and say

- Children look at the colours for a moment or two. Tell them to listen.
- Play the first part of the Tape. Children point to colours and repeat in the pauses.

Tapescript

Narrator: Topic 3. Lesson 7. Activity 1. Listen, point and say.

Voice: Pink. [pause]

Purple. [pause]

Orange. [pause]

Brown. [pause]

Grey. [pause]

- Put the colour Flashcards on the board in the same sequence as in the book. Point to each one in order. The class says the colours.

- Play the next part of the Tape. Children point in their books and name the colours.

Tapescript

Narrator: Now listen again, point and say with me.

Pink, purple, orange, brown, grey.

[pause]

Pink, purple, orange, brown, grey.

[pause]

- Children practise saying the colours in pairs. They take turns to point and ask *What colour is it?* Listen to as many pairs as possible.

- If children find the question difficult, they can point to the colours and name them. Some children may need extra help to name the colours. Put these children together in a group and practise the colours with them.

2 Listen, look and say

- Hold up the alphabet Flashcard for the letter *v*, with the picture showing. Say *van*. Class repeats. Turn the card to show the letter *v*. Class names it.

- Show the letter. Say *v*, /v/. Show the picture. Say *van*. Show them again. Class says *v*, /v/, *van*.

- Do the same with the *w* and *x* Flashcards.

- Children look in their books at the three pictures. Tell them to listen and look at the first letter and picture. Play the sequence for *v*. Children repeat in the pauses. Stop the Tape.

- Point to the van in the book. Prompt children to point. Check they have the correct picture. Say *v*, /v/, *van* again, pausing for the children to repeat as on the Tape.

- Follow the procedure in the same way for *w* and *x*.

- Play the Tape without stopping. Children point in their books and repeat.

Tapescript

Narrator: Topic 3. Lesson 7. Activity 2. Listen, look and say.

Voice: v. [pause] /v/. [pause] Van. [pause]

w. [pause] /w/. [pause] Watch. [pause]

x. [pause] /ks/. [pause] Box. [pause]

Extension activity

- Play one of the *Colours games* (see Games 8 and 9 on page 9) using the new colours.

 page 43

1 Write

For detailed guidance notes on handwriting practice, see the teaching notes on page 19 (Workbook, Lesson 1, Activity 1).

- Children write over the dotted lines inside the letter *v* next to the exemplar, following the arrows in order.

- They write over the tinted letters *v* starting at the dot.

- They complete the rows starting at the dot.

- They write a row independently, keeping within the guidelines.

- They do the same for the letter *V*.

Lesson 8

Performance indicators

Children will be able to:
- ask about numbers of items
- use the plural s
- write w and W correctly.

New language

How many (cats)?

Review language

brown, grey, orange, pink, purple
It's pink and yellow.

Bring to the lesson

- the Tape
- real classroom objects for counting
- the Flashcards for pink, purple, brown, orange and grey
- 7 or 8 Flashcards of different coloured items

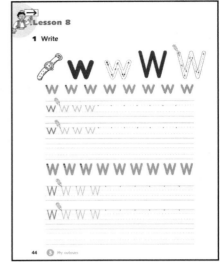

PB page 41   WB page 44

Warm-up

- Use the colour Flashcards to revise the new colours.
- Choose seven or eight Flashcards that use the new colours.
- Ask, e.g. What colour is the fan? Prompt, e.g. *It's blue and grey. Ask What is it?* Prompt, e.g. *It's a brown and orange lion.*

Presentation

- Hold up a book and say *1 book.* Class repeats.
- Hold up two books. Say *2 books,* making the *s* ending clear. Class repeats.
- Do the same with one pencil and two pencils.
- If your class needs more practice with hearing and repeating the *s* plural ending, continue with pens, bags, balls, etc.
- Hold up two books and ask *How many books?* Be ready to give the answer yourself: 2. Say *2 books.* Class repeats.

- Hold up, e.g. two balls. Ask *How many balls?* Elicit *2 balls.*
- Hold up three pencils and ask again.
- Continue with two to four of any one item until the class has understood the new question and are sounding the plural *s*.

PB page 41

1 Listen, find and answer

- Let children study the picture in their books for a minute or two.
- Play the first part of the Tape. Children listen to the questions and find the items in the picture. They listen to the answer and repeat it.

Tapescript

Narrator: Topic 3. Lesson 8. Activity 1. Listen, find and answer.

Child 1: How many trees? [pause]

Child 2: 3 trees. [pause]

Child 1: How many goats? [pause]

Child 2: 1 goat. [pause]

Child 1: How many apples? [pause]

Child 2: 8 apples. [pause]

- Check through the activity with the whole class. Ask the first question and prompt the answer from a child. Hold up your book and count the trees *1, 2, 3*.

- Ask again *How many trees?* The whole class replies *3 trees*.

- Do the same with the other two questions.

- Play the second part of the Tape. This time, the children answer the question immediately, then listen to the answer on the Tape to check.

Tapescript

Narrator: Now listen again and answer

Child 1: How many trees? [pause]

Child 2: 3 trees. [pause]

Child 1: How many goats? [pause]

Child 2: 1 goat. [pause]

Child 1: How many apples? [pause]

Child 2: 8 apples. [pause]

2 Talk

- Hold up your book, point to one of the cats and say *Look. What is it?* Elicit *It's a cat,* or *It's a white cat.* Ask *How many cats?* Elicit *4 cats*.

- Point and ask questions about boys, planes, birds, cats, vans and dogs.

- When children can answer confidently, let them ask and answer *How many ... ?* in pairs. Listen to as many pairs as you can.

- Children who find this activity difficult may just answer with the number.

Extension activity

Use the picture to ask a variety of questions of individuals around the class.

- Point and ask *What is it?* Elicit *It's a van/dog/goat/ plane/cat/tree*.

- Ask *What colour is the van/dog/goat/plane/cat/tree?* Elicit answers.

 page 44

1 Write

For detailed guidance notes on handwriting practice, see the teaching notes on page 19 (Workbook, Lesson 1, Activity 1).

- Children write over the dotted lines inside the letter *w* next to the exemplar, following the arrows in order.

- They write over the tinted letters *w* starting at the dot.

- They complete the rows starting at the dot.

- They write a row independently, keeping within the guidelines.

- They do the same for the letter *W*.

Lesson 9

Performance indicators

Children will be able to:
- follow and act out a story
- colour a picture by dictation
- count items and write the numbers.

New language

lovely, teacher

Review language

How many ... ?
Wash your hands.
Dry your hands.
Clean the board.
Wipe the table.

Bring to the lesson

- the Tape
- different numbers of real classroom items to practise *How many ... ?* (see Warm-up)
- a bowl, a towel, a cloth and a board rubber for Presentation and Activity 2, Act it out

Preparation

Check to see what coloured pencils children have for Workbook Activity 1. Adapt the listening script as necessary, substituting available colours.

PB **page 42**   WB **page 45**

Warm-up

- Hold up several pencils. Ask *How many pencils?* Class replies. Repeat with one or two other objects.

- Divide the class into two. Give a child in Team A several of one item to hold up. Prompt Team A to ask Team B, e.g. *How many books?* Team B replies together.

- Change over, so that Team B holds the objects and asks the question.

- Continue using items children can see and name and that you can find easily, e.g. rulers, pens, pencil cases, crayons, balls, etc. Include one of some items so children remember the singular form has no final *s*.

Presentation

- Revise the instructions children learned for cleaning up: *Wipe the table. Clean the board. Wash your hands. Dry your hands.* Bring four children forward and give them instructions in turn. Indicate the items you have brought in as appropriate. Children use them to show the action.

- Mime each action and say the instruction. Class repeats and follows your action.

PB **page 42**

1 Listen and read

- Children look at the pictures. Point out the objects in the drawings that the children have painted for their teacher. Ask *What is it?* and *What colour is it?*

- Ask about the jug *What colour is it now?* Ask what colour they think it should be.

- Ask children what they think is happening in the story.

- Play the Tape. Children listen and follow in their books.

Tapescript

Narrator:	Topic 3. Lesson 9. Activity 1. Listen and read.
Leila/Rania:	For our teacher, Miss Nadia.
Leila:	Look!
Rania:	Oh, no!
Leila:	Wipe the table!
Rania:	Wash the jug!
Miss Nadia:	Thank you, girls. They are lovely! Now clean the board and wash your hands.

● Explain *lovely* and *teacher*. Read out the speech bubbles. Children repeat.

● Play the Tape again. Children follow in their books and repeat in the pause.

2 Act it out

● Hold up your book, point to the pictures and say the words. Prompt the class to follow and join in.

● Do this again until you are certain children can follow the picture sequence and say the words confidently.

● Children practise the dialogue in groups of three, pointing to the correct picture as they speak. Go round and listen to some of them.

● One or two groups can speak in front of the class using the items you have brought in. They can use pictures they have coloured in their Workbooks, or their own paintings for the first scene.

Extension activity

● Practise *How many + (colour) + (noun)?* Use coloured socks (Topic 2, Lesson 10).

● Put, e.g. three red, two green and one white sock on the board. Ask *How many red socks?* Elicit *3 red socks*.

● Ask about the other socks.

● Put up different numbers of blue, yellow and black socks and ask again.

 page 45

1 Listen and colour

● Children listen and colour the parts of the umbrella according to this script: *Number 1 is orange, number 2 is grey, number 3 is pink, number 4 is purple, number 5 is brown.*

● Children should be able to name the umbrella. If they say *It's 'a' umbrella*, repeat the sentence correctly without drilling. A/An is taught in Topic 4, Lesson 8.

2 Count and write

● Children look in the large picture and try to find the items in the small pictures below. They count them and write the numbers in the boxes.

Answers

2 planes, 6 birds, 8 balloons, 4 trees, 3 balls, 7 cats

Lesson 10

Performance indicators

Children will be able to:
- sing a song
- recognise and say the sound of the letters *y* and *z*
- match the phonic sounds /j/ and /z/, to the written letters *y* and *z*
- write *x* and *X* correctly.

New language

The words in the song.

Review language

colours

Bring to the lesson

- the Tape
- the alphabet Flashcards for m–x
- the alphabet Flashcards for y and z

Preparation

Make 10 balloon shapes from paper or card (see Extension activities).

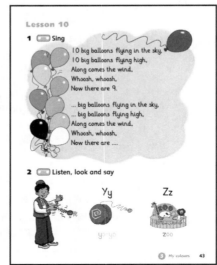

PB **page 43**   WB **page 46**

Warm-up

- Show the class some alphabet Flashcard letters from *m* to *x*. See if they can say the sound and then name the object without seeing it. If necessary, turn the Flashcard to show the picture.

Presentation

- Draw ten balloons on the board. Children count them. Number each one. Ask *How many balloons?* Elicit *10 balloons*.

- Help the class understand the song from Activity 1 using English, if possible. Teach the following actions:

  10 big (hold arms out wide) *balloons flying in the sky* (point upwards),

  10 big balloons flying high (look upwards and shade eyes with hand),

  Along comes the wind (make whistling wind sound),

  Whoosh, whoosh, (flap your hands at 10th balloon on the board)

  Now there are nine. (rub out the 10th balloon)

PB **page 43**

 1 Sing

- Children look at the picture in their books. Count the balloons with them.

- Tell them to listen. Play the Tape and stop after the first verse.

- Say the words of the first verse phrase by phrase. Use the actions as you speak. This will help children remember new words and recognise others they already know. Children repeat and do the same actions.

- Help children to say the verse and do the actions all the way through.

- Play the Tape again. Children sing along. Concentrate on the easy parts first (*10 big balloons* and *Whoosh, whoosh, etc*). Children will gain confidence as they practise.

Narrator: Topic 3. Lesson 10. Activity 1. Sing.

Voices: 10 big balloons flying in the sky,

10 big balloons flying high,

Along comes the wind,

Whoosh, whoosh,

Now there are 9.

… big balloons flying in the sky,

… big balloons flying high,

Along comes the wind,

Whoosh, whoosh,

Now there are …

- Sing two or three more verses with actions. At the end of each verse, rub off the board the balloon that has blown away. Point to the number that will start the next verse.

Extension activity

- Bring 10 children forward to be the 10 balloons and 10 more to be the wind.

- The balloon children stand in a line facing the class. The wind children stand in a group near the first balloon.

- All the children sing the song and do the actions. On *Whoosh, whoosh* the first child in the wind group runs across to the 10th balloon and takes him/her away (they both sit back in their places).

- Do the same for each verse until the last wind child takes away the last balloon. (The last line of the last verse is *Now there are none*.)

Note:

- Children can make ten numbered, coloured balloons as in the book and hold them up in the song. This could be sung to another class or parents at the end of term. (Use the balloons to practise *What colour is it?* and *What number is it?* in class time.)

- If space is restricted in your classroom, make numbered balloon shapes and stick them on the board. Remove them, or ask a child to remove them during each verse.

2 Listen, look and say

- Hold up the alphabet Flashcard for the letter *y*, with the picture showing. Say *yo-yo*. Class repeats. Turn the card to show the letter y. Class names it.

- Show the letter. Say *y, /j/*. Show the picture. Say *yo-yo*. Show them again. Class says *y, /j/, yo-yo*.

- Do the same with the *z* Flashcard.

- Children look in their books. Tell them to look at the first letter and picture. Play the sequence for *y* on the Tape. They repeat in the pauses. Stop the Tape.

- Point to the yo-yo in the book. Prompt children to point. Check they have the correct picture. Say *y, /y/, yo-yo*. Children repeat.

- Follow the procedure in the same way for *z*.

- Play the Tape without stopping. Children point in their books and repeat.

Tapescript

Narrator: Topic 3. Lesson 10. Activity 2. Listen, look and say.

Voice: y. [pause] /j/. [pause] Yo-yo. [pause]

z. [pause] /z/. [pause] Zoo. [pause]

WB **page 46**

1 Write

For detailed guidance notes on handwriting practice, see the teaching notes on page 19 (Workbook, Lesson 1, Activity 1).

- Children write over the dotted lines inside the letter *x* next to the exemplar, following the arrows in order.

- They write over the tinted letters *x* starting at the dot.

- They complete the rows starting at the dot.

- They write a row independently, keeping within the guidelines.

- They do the same for the letter *X*.

Lesson 11 – Review

Performance indicators

Children will be able to:
- use and understand the language taught in Lessons 1–10
- write y and Y correctly
- write z and Z correctly.

Review language

Letters and exemplar objects s–x

Bring to the lesson

- the Tape
- the Flashcards for all the items on page 44 of the Pupil's Book (bag, balloon, book, fan, pen, van, yo-yo, watch)
- the alphabet Flashcards for s, t, u, x and z

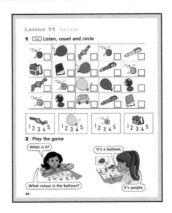

 PB page 44   **WB** pages 47 and 48

Warm-up

- Sing the balloon song from Lesson 10.

Presentation

- Write these letters, spaced out on the board: b, f, p, v, w and y.

- Show the class the Flashcards for each item in the grid on page 44 one at a time. Class names the object.

- Choose a child to place each Flashcard by the correct letter on the board, or to say the initial letter while a child at the front places the Flashcard.

PB page 44

1 Listen, count and circle

- Children look at the pictures for a minute or two. While they do so, draw simple outlines of a pen, a book and a van on the board. Write the numbers 1, 2, 3, 4 and 5 underneath each one.

- Hold up your book and point to the grid. Ask *How many pens?* Elicit *3 pens.* Circle the number 3 under the pen you drew on the board.

- Ask *How many books/vans?* Elicit answers and circle the number under the pictures on the board.

- Point out the four pictures below the grid and tell the children to listen. Play the Tape. Stop the Tape after each question, if necessary, to give children time to count and circle the correct number under each picture.

Tapescript

Narrator: Topic 3. Lesson 11. Activity 1. Listen, count and circle.

Voice: How many watches? [pause]

How many balloons? [pause]

How many yo-yos? [pause]

How many bags? [pause]

- Check answers by asking individuals.
- Finally ask *How many fans?* Elicit *2*.

Answers

2 watches, 4 balloons, 5 yo-yos, 1 bag

2 Play the game

- Bring a child to the front with his/her book and a pencil. Say *Point to a picture.* Child points.

- Say *Tick the box.* (Demonstrate this on the board.)

- Tell the child to point to the picture again. Ask *What is it?* Prompt e.g. *It's a balloon.* Ask *What colour is the balloon?* Child replies, e.g. *It's purple.*

- Turn your book to the class, point and say *It's a purple balloon.* Show the class you are looking for the picture of the purple balloon. Find it, and tick it so the class can see.

- You and the child hold up your books. Show that the same pictures are ticked.

- Do this with other children and pictures until the class has grasped the game.

- Children continue the activity in pairs. They take turns to ask and answer until all the boxes are ticked.

Extension activities

- Children play the *Find the … game.* The first child says e.g. *Find the blue watch.* The other child looks for the correct picture in the grid in Activity 1 and points to it. Then they change over.

- Children play the *What is it? game.* The first child points to a picture in the grid in Activity 1 and asks the question. The other child replies, e.g. *It's a blue yo-yo.*

 pages 47 and 48

1 Write

For detailed guidance notes on handwriting practice, see the teaching notes on page 19 (Workbook, Lesson 1, Activity 1).

- Children write over the dotted lines inside the letter *y* next to the exemplar, following the arrows in order.

- They write over the tinted letters *y* starting at the dot.

- They complete the rows starting at the dot.

- They write a row independently, keeping within the guidelines.

- They do the same for the letter *Y*.

2 Write

- Children practise writing *z* and *Z* as in Activity 1, above.

Lesson 12

Performance indicators

Children will be able to:
- name the ten colours
- count from 1–10
- describe an object by colour
- identify a group of objects by number and colour.

New language

count

Review language

Vocabulary and structures from Topics 1–3

Bring to the lesson

- the Flashcards for colours
- the Flashcard for bird
- the green and red circle cards (from Topic 2, Lesson 10)
- a cut-out bird shape for each child

Preparation

- Use Resources pages 162 and 168 to make enough bird shape for all the children in the class to have one each.
- Check to see what coloured pencils children have for Workbook Activity 1. Adapt the listening script as necessary, substituting available colours.

 page 45   **page 49**

Warm-up

- Divide the class into five or six numbered teams. Play the *Stop and go game* (see page 9). You can play this as an elimination game: any team that does not follow the instruction properly or quickly enough must sit down.

Presentation

- Put all the colour Flashcards on your desk. Divide the class into between four and six teams. Give each team a colour, e.g. blue team, red team, etc.

- Hold up a colour Flashcard. That team must stand up at once, say the colour together and sit down again.

- Hold up each colour at least once, in any order. Start slowly, then go more quickly.

- After each team has stood up several times, change the colours around between the teams and add in any colours which were not used the first time.

 page 45

1 Play the Flashcard game

- Children look carefully at the picture in their books for a moment or two.

- Hold up your book, point to, e.g. a purple bird and ask the class or an individual *What is it?* Elicit *It's a (purple) bird*. (Ask *What colour is it?* if that is not in the first answer.)

- Help children to ask about number. Say *How many … ?* and hold up the purple Flashcard and the bird Flashcard. Prompt the class to say *purple birds*. Check that they add the plural *s*. Say *Count the purple birds*. Demonstrate counting with the class. Prompt the answer *Six purple birds*.

- Repeat this with one or two other colour birds.

- Children can continue the activity in pairs. Alternatively continue with the whole class.

88 **3** *My colours*

- If some children find this difficult, choose one of these easier activities for them to do in pairs:

Activity 1 Child A points to a bird and asks *What is it?*

Child B answers. *It's a (purple) bird.*

Activity 2 Child A points to a bird and asks *What colour is it?*

Child B answers *Purple./It's purple.*

Activity 3 Both children take turns to point and say *It's orange. It's brown*, etc.

Activity 4 Child A points to a colour bird and says, e.g. *Grey*.

Child B counts all the grey birds and says the number.

Answers

There are 6 purple birds, 8 yellow birds, 4 orange birds, 2 brown birds, 3 grey birds, 1 black and white bird, and 3 blue and pink birds.

Extension activities

- Make your own class poster.

- Give out one prepared bird shape to each child. They colour them in one or two colours. You may need to tell them which colours to use.

- Make sure you don't end up with more than ten birds in any one colour. Try to have different numbers of birds in each colour.

- Arrange them on a large sheet of paper and stick them on.

- Keep the poster to use for counting practice and naming all the colours.

 page 49

- This page can be used a test to check on class progress in work covered in Topic 3. Give children a fixed length of time to complete each activity.

- Prepare examples of exercises 2 and 3 so that children know what to do. Activity 2, draw several of a simple object on the board, e.g. five apples. Say *Count*. Count the apples with the class then say *Write the number* and write number 5 below your drawing. For activity 3, draw a simple outline on the board, e.g. a ring. Write letters, e.g. *r*, *f* and *t* below. Elicit from the class the correct initial letter and circle it.

- Alternatively, use this page as normal Workbook activities and explain each task in turn, keeping the whole class working together.

1 Listen and colour

- Children colour according to this script: *Listen and colour the vans. Number 1, orange. [pause] Number 2, grey. [pause] Number 3, brown.*

2 Count, write and say

- Children count each group of objects and write the number in the box. If you wish, you can go round and ask children to say the numbers, to make this a partly oral test.

Answers

8, 5, 10, 7

3 Circle the right letter

- Children look at the pictures and the letters below. They circle the letter that begins the name of each object.

4 My favourite things

In this topic pupils:

- name eight new toys (Lessons 1 and 7)
- listen and follow colouring/drawing instructions (Lessons 1 and 5)
- ask about an object and reply in the affirmative and negative (Lesson 2)
- write initial letters, trace and write words (Lessons 2–12)
- say all the alphabet letter sounds, name exemplars and read letters (Lesson 4)
- describe the size of objects (Lesson 5)

- read *ball, kite, bat, doll, teddy, yo-yo, train, car, boat* and *bike* (Lessons 1, 2, 7 and 8)
- join numbers in sequence (Lesson 7)
- read and use *a* and *an* correctly (Lesson 8)
- read a story and learn a rhyme (Lesson 9)
- sing a song (Lesson 10)
- identify aurally the initial letters in the consonant/vowel/consonant words cat, hat, hen and pen (Lessons 7 and 10)
- practise and consolidate (Lessons 6, 11 and 12)

Lesson 1

Performance indicators

Children will be able to:
- name four new toys
- read *ball, kite* and *bat*
- listen and follow colouring instructions.

New language

bat, kite, doll, teddy

Reading words

ball, kite, bat,

Review language

colours
alphabet sounds and exemplars

Bring to the lesson

- the Tape
- the Flashcards for ball, bat, kite, doll, teddy, yo-yo
- word cards for *ball, bat* and *kite*
- the Flashcards for colours
- the alphabet Flashcards

Preparation

- Use Resources page 162 to make word cards for *ball, bat* and *kite*.
- Check to see what coloured pencils children have for Workbook Activity 1. Adapt the listening script as necessary, substituting available colours.

 page 46   **page 50**

Warm-up

- Use the alphabet Flashcards to revise all the letter sounds and exemplars.
- Use Flashcards to revise all the colours.

Presentation

- Show Flashcards of the ball and yo-yo. Children name them.
- Introduce the new words in the usual way. Show the bat Flashcard. Say *bat*. Class repeats. Do this a few times.
- Introduce *kite* and *doll* in the same way.
- Hold up the three Flashcards in any order. Children say the words. Introduce *teddy*. Class repeats.
- Show the four new objects in any order. Class says the words.

page 46

 1 Listen and find

- Children look at the pictures in their books for a moment or two. Tell them to listen. Play the Tape.

Tapescript

Narrator: Topic 4. My favourite things. Lesson 1. Activity 1. Listen and find.

Child 1: Find the bat. It's green. [pause]

Child 2: Find the teddy. It's brown. [pause]

Child 1: Find the kite. It's yellow and purple. [pause]

Child 2: Now find the doll. It's pink. [pause]

- If necessary, stop the Tape and check that children can find each object. Hold up your book, repeat the instruction and point to the object.
- If your class is confident with this activity, play the Tape without stopping, then play it a second time for children to check together in pairs.

2 Play the game

- Point to the ball in Activity 1. Ask *What is it?* Elicit *It's a ball.* (If children answer *It's a grey and white ball*, move straight on to the other toys.)

- Ask *What colour is it?* Elicit *It's grey and white.* Say *Yes. It's a grey and white … .* Elicit *ball*. Prompt the class to repeat *It's a grey and white ball*.
- Point to the bat. Ask *What is it?* If a child answers *It's a green bat*, simply say *Yes. It's a green … ,* and elicit *bat* from the rest of the class.
- Go through the rest of the toys in the same way.
- Begin the description of one or two of the toys and let the class complete the sentence with the correct toy, e.g. *It's a brown … .* Class replies *teddy.*
- Children work in pairs. Child A describes the colour of a toy, and child B names it.

Reading: *ball, bat* and *kite*

- Introduce the first word.

  1 Hold up the Flashcard of the ball. Class names it.

  2 Hold up the alphabet Flashcard for the letter *b*. Class says /b/.

  3 Stick the letter and picture Flashcards beside each other on the board. Point and say /b/, *ball*. Class repeats.

  4 Stick the word card for ball on the board. Point to it and say *ball* again. Class repeats.

  5 Hold up your book and point to the ball. Name it and point to the word below. Check children are pointing to it. Say *ball*. Class repeats. Point to the word on the board. Class reads the word.

- Introduce *bat* and *kite* in the same way.
- Point to the words on the board in any order. Class reads.

Extension activity

- Stick the word cards for *ball, bat* and *kite* on the board jumbled up with the matching Flashcards. Ask individual children to match the words and pictures. Ask the class if the matching is correct each time.

page 50

1 Listen, find and colour

- Children look at the pictures. Prompt the class to name the objects. Children point in their books. Check they have the correct object. Alternatively, read the script straight away. Teacher's script (pause after each colour for children to colour in): Find the bat. It's red. Find the yo-yo. It's pink. Find the doll. It's brown. Find the kite. It's blue and yellow. Find the ball. It's black and white. Find the teddy. It's grey.

Lesson 2

Performance indicators

Children will be able to:
- ask about an object
- reply in the affirmative and negative
- read *doll*, *teddy* and *yo-yo*
- read and join six words to pictures
- write initial letters for six words

New language

Is it a ... ?
yes, no

Review language

bat, kite, doll, teddy

Bring to the lesson

- the Tape
- word cards for *doll*, *teddy* and *yo-yo*
- the Flashcards for toys

Preparation

Use Resources page 162 to make word cards for *doll*, *teddy* and *yo-yo*.

PB page 47   WB page 51

Warm-up

- Revise the new words from Lesson 1. Either show each Flashcard and elicit the name of the object, or play a Flashcard game.
- Play the *Find number … . What is it?* game (see Game 6, page 9).

Presentation

- Hold up the doll Flashcard. Ask *What is it?* Prompt *It's a doll.* Say *Is it a bat? No. It's a doll.*
- Show the bat. Ask *Is it a bat?* Say *Yes. It's a bat.*
- Show the teddy and kite Flashcards and ask questions to elicit *Yes* or *No* answers. Children may add *It's a …* following their answer. If they do not, you can ask *What is it?* to practise the new words.

PB page 47

1 Listen and say

- Children look at the pictures for a moment. Tell them to listen. Play the Tape.
- Pause the Tape after each Yes/No answer. Say, e.g. *Find the doll. What number is it?* Children look, find the correct picture and say *Number 9.* Continue in the same way with the rest of the Tape.
- Play the Tape again. Pause after each question. Children give the answer before the voice on the Tape and again after the signal.

Tapescript

Narrator: Topic 4. Lesson 2. Activity 1. Listen and say.

[Sound effect: doll says *Hello* and laughs]

Child 1: Is it a doll?

Child 2: Yes. [ping] [pause]

[Sound effect: mechanical dog growls]

Child 1: Is it a cat?

Child 2: No. It's a dog. [ping] [pause]

[Sound effect: ball bouncing]

Child 1: Is it a ball?

Child 2: Yes. [ping] [pause]

[Sound effect: kite, wind, birdsong]

Child 1: Is it a yo-yo?

Child 2: No. It's a kite. [ping] [pause]

2 Play the game

- Use the pictures in Activity 1 to check recognition of all the objects. Say *Find number 5. What is it?* Elicit answers from the whole class. You can also ask individuals or rows of children to answer.

- Play the *Is it a … ? game* with the whole class, prompting answers as necessary. Say, e.g. *Number 2. Is it a cat?* Elicit *Yes. (It's a cat.).* Say, e.g. *Number 4. Is it a dog?* Elicit *No. It's a kite.*

- When the class is used to finding pictures and answering with your help, divide the class into two or more teams and ask questions of individual children.

- When children become confident with this activity they can continue in pairs.

Reading: *doll, teddy* and *yo-yo*

- Introduce the first word.

  1 Hold up the Flashcard of the doll. Class names it.

  2 Hold up the alphabet Flashcard for the letter *d*. Class says /d/.

  3 Stick the letter and picture Flashcards beside each other on the board. Point and say /d/, *doll*. Class repeats.

  4 Stick the word card for *doll* on the board. Point to it and say *doll* again. Class repeats.

  5 Hold up your book and point to the doll on page 46. Name it and point to the word below. Check children are pointing to it. Say *doll*. Class repeats. Point to the word on the board. Class reads the word.

- Introduce *teddy* and *yo-yo* in the same way.

- Point to the words on the board in any order. Class reads.

- Stick or write up the three reading words from Lesson 1 (*ball, bat* and *kite*). Revise them using Flashcards if necessary.

- Point to the six words in any order. Class reads.

Extension activity

- Practise *Is it a … ?* questions and prompt *Yes/No* answers from the class. Show real objects or Flashcards of objects that children can name.

- Play it as a team game. Teams take turns to show an object and ask the question.

 page 51

1 Write and join

Note: If you wish, leave the word cards and Flashcards from the Reading activity on the board while the class does these two exercises. If your class is confident, you could remove the pictures. To check the children's work when they have finished, ask individuals to place the correct Flashcard by each word on the board. Children look in their books to see if they have joined them correctly.

- Children write the initial letter of each word. They read the words and draw lines joining them to the correct picture.

2 Trace, write and join

- Children draw over the dotted shapes to make a complete outline picture. They then write over the initial letter of each of the words, read them and join them to the correct picture.

Lesson 3

Performance indicators

Children will be able to:
- express need for something
- name four household items
- match shapes and capital/small letters
- write initial letters to new words.

New language

I need a ... .
plate, spoon, cup, glass

Review language

1, 2, 3, 4, 5, 6
bat, teddy, doll, kite, yo-yo, ball

Bring to the lesson

- the Tape
- a plate, a spoon, a cup and a glass
- word cards and Flashcards for toys

Preparation

Place the Flashcards for numbers 1 to 6 around the classroom.

PB page 48   WB page 52

Warm-up

- Revise the six words for toys. Show a picture Flashcard. Class says the word. Show the word card. Class reads. Show word cards in any order. Class reads.

- Stick the toy Flashcards on the board. Stick the word cards below them in any order. Individuals come forward to match word cards and Flashcards. Leave these up for the Presentation activity.

Presentation

- Point out the number Flashcards around the classroom. Say *I need number 1.* Then, e.g. *Dina, bring me number 1, please.* When the child has brought it, stick it next to the first paired Flashcard and word card.

- Say *I need number 2.* Ask a child to bring it to you and stick it next to a Flashcard and word card. Continue with the other numbers so that each pair of cards is numbered.

- Quickly do a question and answer activity with the class. Say *Number 4. What is it?* Children answer. (Leave everything on the board for the Extension activity.)

- Show the household items you have brought in. Use them to present the vocabulary (*plate, spoon, cup* and *glass*) in the usual way.

PB page 48

1 Listen, find and say

- Children look at the picture of Leila playing. Point out the pictures below. Help the class to name each one.

- Children find the new items in the big picture. Name each one. Class repeats.

- Play the Tape. Children listen and point to the items as Leila mentions them.

Tapescript

Narrator: Topic 4. Lesson 3. Activity 1. Listen, find and say.

Leila: I need a plate. [pause]
Now I need a cup. [pause]
And now I need a spoon. [pause] Mum!

Mum: Yes, dear.

Leila: Please give me a glass. [pause]

Mum: Here you are.

Leila: Thank you.

- Hold up your book, point and say, e.g. *I need a plate*. Children point in their books and repeat. Continue with the other items.

- Play the Tape a second time. Children look in their books, point and repeat each item.

2 Play the game

- Play the *I need a ... Memory chain game*. Line up the household items (plate, spoon, cup and glass) on your desk. Bring three children to your desk. Point to the first object. Say, e.g. *I need a glass*. Prompt the first child to repeat and then add on the next object, e.g. *I need a glass and a cup*. Prompt the next child to name three items. The last child should say all four items.

- Children work in pairs, taking turns to point in their books and add on the next object. Go around listening to some of them.

- Tell children to close their books. Prompt a child to say, e.g. *I need a plate*. Prompt another to say the sentence and add on an item. Continue until the four items have been added. Do this again once or twice.

Extension activity

- Remove the toy Flashcards from the board, leaving just number Flashcards and the six reading words. Say a number. Children read the word next to it.

- Play in two or more teams. Alternatively, ask individuals to answer so you can check on children's progress.

 page 52

1 Join and write

- Children draw lines between matching shapes and write the capital letter in the blank.

2 Write and join

- Children write the initial letter of each word and join it to the correct picture.

Lesson 4

Performance indicators

Children will be able to:
- say all the alphabet letter sounds and name the exemplars
- recognise the order of letters in the alphabet.

Review language

the alphabet and exemplars

Bring to the lesson

- the alphabet Flashcards

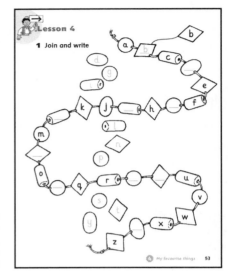

PB **page 49**   WB **page 53**

Warm-up

- Sing *Red socks, Green socks* from Topic 2, Lesson 10.

Presentation

- Practise the sound of each letter of the alphabet in order. Show the first Flashcard. Children say *apple*. Turn the card and show the letter side. Children say /æ/. Prompt them for the first few letters, if necessary. Then let the class continue alone.

- Do this again. Go a little faster if your class is confident with the letter sounds. Do this for the whole alphabet.

 page 49

1 Point and say

- Hold up the alphabet Flashcards one at a time with the letter sides facing the class. Children say the sound.

- Children point in their books at each letter in order and say the sound.

- Check that children can say the sounds correctly. Use any or all of these methods:

  1 Divide the class into rows or groups. Show a letter. Children say the sound. If children are not confident, ask the whole class to repeat.

  2 Show a letter. Choose an individual to say the sound. Class repeats.

  3 Show the whole class a letter. The class says the sound

2 Play the game

- Show the class how to play. Hold up any alphabet Flashcard with the picture side facing the class. Name the object. Turn the Flashcard round and elicit the sound. Do this with two or three different Flashcards.

- Hold up another alphabet Flashcard with the picture side facing the class. Name the object and elicit the sound without turning the Flashcard round. Do this several times until the class is confident with the activity.

- Divide the class into three or more teams, rows or small groups. Play the game using the alphabet Flashcards. Add in the Flashcards for the new words the children have learnt.

- Show a Flashcard to Team A. They name the object. Team B says the initial sound.

- Show Team B a picture. They name it and Team C says the initial sound.

- Continue in this way with as many teams as you have. Give each team several turns until the whole class is confident.

Extension activities

- Children who need practice with naming sounds can work with the alphabet Flashcards. They name the object and say the sound of the initial letter. They turn the Flashcard over to check. Monitor the progress of these children as they do the activity.

 page 53

1 Join and write

- Children look at the string of beads. Point out that there are some gaps.

- Children look at the tinted letters and join them to the correct space.

- They write over the tinted letter and then write it in the space.

Lesson 5

Performance indicators

Children will be able to:
- describe the size of objects
- draw from dictated instructions
- count objects and write the number.

New language

big, small,

Review language

bird, tree, nest, plane, sun
very

Bring to the lesson

- the Tape
- the Flashcards for bird, tree, nest, plane and sun
- two or three pairs of big and small objects that children can name, e.g. balls, keys, boxes, books, bags, etc

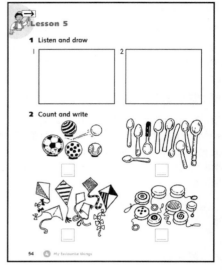

PB **page 50** WB **page 54**

Warm-up

- Sing one or two verses of *Ten big balloons* from Topic 3, Lesson 10, with the actions.

- Show the Flashcards for the objects the children will hear on the Tape: plane, bird, nest, sun and tree. Children name them.

Presentation

- Show, e.g. a big ball. Elicit *ball*. Say *It's a big ball*. Show a small ball. Say *It's a small ball*.

- Hold up the big ball. Say *big*. Children repeat. Do the same with the small ball and *small*.

- Hold up the first ball. Say *It's a big ball*. Children repeat. Do the same with the small ball.

- Repeat with one or two other pairs of objects.

PB **page 50**

1 Listen and find

- Explain that Samir has painted this picture. Ask the class to name the objects in the picture.

- Tell children to listen to Samir and Karim. Play the Tape. Children point to the objects as they hear them mentioned on the Tape.

Tapescript

Narrator: Topic 4. Lesson 5. Activity 1. Listen and find.

Samir: Look at the plane. It's small. [pause]

Karim: The bird is big. [pause]

And look at the nest. It's very big. [pause]

Samir: [laugh] Oh, yes. The sun is small. [pause]

Karim: Look at the tree. It's a small tree. [pause]

- Play the Tape again. Prompt children to point to the object in their books in the pauses and say *It's small* or *It's big*.

2 Point and say

● Hold up your book. Point to the first picture. Ask *What is it?* Children look in their books. Prompt *Cat/It's a cat.* Ask *Is it a big cat?* Elicit *No. It's small./It's a small cat.*

● Point to the next picture and ask *What is it?* Prompt *It's a big dog.* Only ask about the size if children do not give it in the answer. Class repeats the full answer.

● Ask about the other pictures and elicit *It's a big teddy. It's a small insect. It's a big goat.*

Extension activity

● Draw some simple big and small pictures of objects on the board, e.g. a cat, a tree, a bird, a bat and a kite.

● Divide the class in two. A child from Team A points to one of the pictures. Team A asks *What is it?* Team B answers, e.g. *It's a small cat.*

 page 54

1 Listen and draw

● Children draw in the two boxes according to your instructions. If you have drawn objects on the board for the Extension activities, leave them for children to copy. If not, put examples on the board now.

● Instruct the children to draw in each box, e.g. *Box 1. Draw a big cat. Box 2. Draw a small bird.*

2 Count and write

● Children count the number of items and write the numbers in the boxes.

Answers
5, 10, 7, 8

Lesson 6

Performance indicators

Children will be able to:
- ask and answer questions about objects
- match and write capital and small letters.

New language

(Extension) *Is it a big teddy?*

Review language

bat, teddy, doll, kite, yo-yo, ball
What is it?
Is it a ball?

Bring to the lesson

- the Flashcards for jug, pen, umbrella, watch and key
- the word cards for bat, ball, doll, kite, teddy and yo-yo
- the flashcards for doll, kite, bat, plane, yo-yo, teddy, ball and van

 page 51   **page 55**

Warm-up

- Use the word cards to practise reading the words *bat, ball, doll, kite, teddy* and *yo-yo*. If your class is confident, show the word cards. Children read.

- If the class needs preparation before reading, follow one of these methods:

  1 Show the Flashcards or real objects in any order. Children name them. Show the word cards in any order. Children read the words

  2 Show each Flashcard or real object and the word card at the same time. Children read the word. Do this a few times then show the word cards only. Children read the words.

Presentation

- Put on the board the Flashcards for jug, pen, umbrella, watch and key. Quickly point to each one. Children name them.

- Tell the class to watch you. Do a mime for one of the objects. Then say to the class *What is it?* When a child gives the right answer say *Yes, it's a ... .* He/She chooses an object and mimes for the others to guess, replying *Yes, it's a ... .* Continue until all the objects have been mimed once.

 page 51

1 Play the Flashcard game

- Children look at the pictures in their books. Place all the same Flashcards face down on your desk. A child comes forward, chooses a Flashcard and shows it only to you. He/She mimes to show what the object is. The others look at the pictures in their books and try to guess what it is, asking *Is it a ... ?*

- This game can also be played in two teams. Choose a child from Team A to mime to Team B. Team A asks *What is it?* Team B guesses *Is it a ... ?*

- For a variation, divide the class into four or more teams. Show a Flashcard to a team. All the children from that team stand up so the rest of the class can see them. They mime the object. The first of the other teams to guess correctly wins the point.

Extension activity

- Tell the class that the objects they mime this time will be big or small. A child chooses a Flashcard from your desk. He/She shows it to you. Whisper to the child *It's big* or *It's small*. The child must mime a big or small object.

- Other children guess, e.g. *Is it a big teddy?* When the correct answer is given, the child replies *Yes, it's a big teddy*.

- This activity can also be done in teams. Award points for good mimes as well as for accurate guessing of the answer.

 page 55

1 Join and say

- Children look at the pictures and join the big and small matching pairs.

- In pairs, children point, ask and answer. Child A points at a picture and asks, e.g. *What is it?* Child B answers, e.g. *It's a small monkey*, etc.

2 Join and write

- Children draw lines between matching shapes and write the capital letter in the blank.

Lesson 7

Performance indicators

Children will be able to:
- name four new toys
- read *train* and *car*
- identify initial letter sounds aurally and write the letters
- join numbers in sequence
- write initial letters and trace words.

New language

train, car, boat, bike

Reading words

train, car

Review language

What is it? It's a ... .

Bring to the lesson

- the Tape
- 6 to 8 Flashcards of things children can mime
- the Flashcards for train, car, boat and bike
- word cards for *train* and *car*

Preparation

- Use Resource pages 162 to make word cards for *train* and *car*.

PB **page 52**   WB **page 56**

Warm-up

- Play a mime game using six to eight Flashcards of objects suitable for miming.

- Where possible, tell children to mime something big or small. Alternatively, after the correct answer is given ask *Is it big/small?*

Presentation

- Use the Flashcards to introduce *train, car, boat* and *bike* in the usual way.

 PB **page 52**

 1 Listen, point, say and play

- Children look at the pictures in their books. Tell them to listen. Play the Tape.

- For the first part of the Tape children point to each object as they hear it. They repeat the word in the pause.

Tapescript

Narrator: Topic 4. Lesson 7. Activity 1. Listen, point and say.

[sound effect: train]

Voice: Train. [pause]

[sound effect: car]

Voice: Car. [pause]

[sound effect: boat]

Voice: Boat. [pause]

[sound effect: bike]

Voice: Bike. [pause]

● For the second part of the Tape children listen to each sound, point to the correct object and complete the sentence in the pause.

Tapescript

Narrator: Now listen, point and say.

[sound effect: boat]

Voice: It's a … . [pause]

[sound effect: car]

Voice: It's a … . [pause]

[sound effect: bike]

Voice: It's a … . [pause]

[sound effect: train]

Voice: It's a … . pause]

● Play the miming game. Bring a child forward. Show the class one of the Flashcards so that the child cannot see. The class mimes the transport. The child watches.

● Stop the mime. Ask the child *What is it?* The child says, e.g. *It's a boat.*

● Do this with the other three Flashcards and three other children. Prompt the class to join in asking *What is it?*

● Bring a different child to the front. Show him/her one of the Flashcards. He/She mimes the item then asks *What is it?* The whole class answers, e.g. *It's a bike.*

● Repeat with other children coming to the front to mime.

 2 Listen, say and write

● Children look at the pictures for a moment. Point to the cat. Class names it. Point to the hat and say *hat*. Make sure children understand the word.

● Play the Tape. Children repeat the word in the pause. They write the initial letter.

Tapescript

Narrator: Topic 4. Lesson 7. Activity 2. Listen, say and write.

Voice: Cat. [pause] Cat. [pause]

Hat. [pause] Hat. [pause]

● Point to the pictures again. Prompt *cat/hat*. Write *cat* on the board and *hat* below it.

● Point to the first letter of *cat* and elicit /k/. Then elicit the whole word.

● Point to the first letter of *hat* and elicit /h/. Then elicit the whole word.

Reading: *train* and *car*

● Introduce the first word.

1 Hold up the Flashcard of the train. Class names it.

2 Hold up the alphabet Flashcard for the letter *t*. Class says /t/.

3 Stick the letter and picture Flashcards beside each other on the board. Point and say /t/, *train*. Class repeats.

4 Stick the word card for *train* on the board. Point to it and say *train* again. Class repeats.

5 Hold up your book and point to the train. Name it and point to the word below. Check children are pointing to it. Say *train*. Class repeats. Point to the word on the board. Class reads the word.

● Introduce *car* in the same way.

● Point to the words on the board in any order. Class reads.

 page 56

1 Join the dots, write and ✓ or ✗

● Children join the dots in the correct order to complete each picture. They read the word below and write over the initial letter. If the word matches the picture they tick in the box. If it does not match the picture they draw a cross.

● If possible, go around checking children's work and helping. Ask children to point and read the words in their books.

Answers
✓, ✗ (kite), ✓

2 Write *b* and complete

● Children write the initial letter *b* for each word and write over the other letters under each picture. Go around checking. Ask children to say each word.

Lesson 8

Performance indicators

Children will be able to:
- use *a* and *an* correctly
- read *boat* and *bike*
- read *a* and *an*
- write four vocabulary words.

New language

an

Reading words

boat, bike

Review language

1, 2, 3, 4, 5, 6, 7, 8, 9, 10
the alphabet exemplars
toys

Bring to the lesson

- the Tape
- the alphabet Flashcards
- the Flashcards for *boat* and *bike*
- word cards for *boat* and *bike*

Preparation

Use Resource page 162 to make word cards for *boat* and *bike*.

 page 53   **page 57**

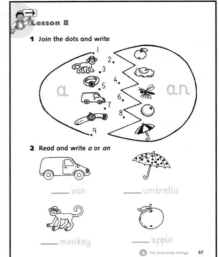

Warm-up

- Revise the numbers 1–10. Children say the numbers. Write them on the board.
- Point in any order. Ask *What number is it?*
- Use classroom objects to revise *How many … ?*, e.g. books, pencils, rulers, rubbers, etc.

Presentation

- Divide the board in two. At the top, write *a* on one side and *an* on the other.
- Write the consonants in order under *a* and the vowels in order under *an*.
- Show a consonant exemplar Flashcard, e.g. ball. Prompt children to name it. Point out *b* on the *a* side of the board. Stick the Flashcard up under the consonants.

- Continue with a few other consonant exemplars from anywhere in the alphabet. Include *monkey* and *van*. Stick the Flashcards on the board with the ball.
- Show the apple Flashcard. Point to the letter *a* under *an*. Say *An apple*. Class repeats. Say *It's an apple*. Class repeats. Stick the picture up under the vowels on the board.
- Do the same with the egg Flashcard and *e*.
- Show two or three more consonant exemplars, then show the insect Flashcard.
- Show the other two vowel exemplars Flashcards (orange and umbrella) in between other consonant exemplars. Children make correct statements, e.g. *It's an orange.*

page 53

1 Listen, find and match

- Children look at the pictures for a moment. Tell them to listen. Play the first part of the Tape. Pause after *a ring*. Point out the lines that are drawn in the picture.

Tapescript

Narrator: Topic 4. Lesson 8. Activity 1. Listen and find.

Voice: Find an apple. [pause]

Now find a ring. [pause]

- Tell children to use their pencils. Play the rest of the Tape. Check that children are drawing matching lines.

Tapescript

Narrator: Now listen, find and match.

Voice: An egg. [pause]

An umbrella. [pause]

A van. [pause]

An orange. [pause]

A monkey. [pause]

An insect. [pause]

- Play the Tape again. Point to each object on the board as it is said. Children repeat in the pauses.

2 Play the game

- Take all the Flashcards off the board, mix them up and put them in a pile.

- Divide the class into two teams. A child from Team A holds up a Flashcard for the whole class to see. Team A asks *What is it?* Team B replies *It's a/an ...* . If they answer correctly, the Flashcard is put on the board on the correct side. Team B wins a point. If the answer is wrong, Team A tries to say it correctly and win the point. Then it is Team B's turn to show a Flashcard and ask the question.

- If your class is confident after a few turns, rub out the vowels and consonants under *a* and *an* on the board.

Extension activities

- Children work in pairs or small groups using the pictures on pages 6 and 7 in the Pupil's Book to point and say *It's a/an ...* .

Reading: *boat* and *bike*

- Introduce the first word.

1 Hold up the Flashcard of the boat. Class names it.

2 Hold up the alphabet Flashcard for the letter *b*. Class says /b/.

3 Stick the letter and picture Flashcards beside each other on the board. Point and say /b/, *boat*. Class repeats.

4 Stick the word card for *boat* on the board. Point to it and say *boat* again. Class repeats.

5 Hold up your book and point to the boat on page 52. Name it and point to the word below. Check children are pointing to it. Say *boat*. Class repeats. Point to the word on the board. Class reads the word.

- Introduce *bike* in the same way.

- Point to the words on the board in any order. Class reads.

page 57

1 Join the dots and write

- Children join the dots in the correct order to complete the crack down the egg.

- Hold up the Workbook and point to *a* on the left side. Ask the class to read the word. Point to each picture in turn and elicit, e.g. *A monkey*, etc.

- Do the same with *an* and the pictures on the right side.

- Children write over the words *a* and *an*.

2 Read and write *a* or *an*

- Children look at the pictures and read the words. They write *a* or *an* in the gap.

- Children then write over the tinted words.

Answers

a van, an umbrella, a monkey, an apple

Lesson 9

Performance indicators

Children will be able to:
- act out a story
- say a rhyme
- write six vocabulary words
- use *a* and *an* correctly.

New language

The words of the song.

Review language

I need ... .
a, an
plate, spoon, cup, glass

Bring to the lesson

- the Tape
- Flashcards for 6–8 objects, including 2–3 with initial vowels

Preparation

Bring in a cup, a spoon, a glass and a plate (all plastic, if possible), for Warm-up.

PB **page 54**   WB **page 58**

Warm-up

- Revise *plate, spoon, cup* and *glass*. Use real items, if possible.

Presentation

- Hold up one of the Flashcards of objects and say, e.g. *I need an egg*. Put the Flashcard on the board. Show another Flashcard and prompt, e.g. *I need a ball*. Put the Flashcard on the board. Continue like this until all the Flashcards are on the board.

- Revise all the words and articles. Point to the Flashcards on the board in any order. Prompt *A ball, An egg*, etc.

PB **page 54**

 ## 1 Listen and read

- Children look at the pictures. Ask them what is happening. Ask who the second boy is (Salama's brother).

- Play the Tape. Children listen and follow in their books.

Tapescript

Narrator: Topic 4. Lesson 9. Activity 1. Listen and read.

Salama: Give me a cup, please. [pause]

I need a spoon. [pause]

Brother: Here you are. [pause]

Salama: Now I need a glass ... and a plate. [pause]

[Crashing sound as all the objects fall]

Oh, dear!

- Hold up your book. Read out the speech bubbles for each picture as you point to them. Children repeat.

- Play the Tape again. Children follow in their books.

- Divide the class into five groups. Each group reads the speech bubble for one picture (two groups read for the second picture).

- If you have more able children, you may wish to let some pairs act out the story, giving the objects but not juggling.

2 A rhyme

- Children look at the picture. Ask *Who it is?* Elicit *Leila*. Can the children say where she is and what she is doing? Write *kitchen* and *door* on the board. Make sure children have understood them, but do not drill them. Do the same with *eating*.

- Play the Tape. Children follow in their books.

Tapescript

Narrator: Topic 4. Lesson 9. Activity 2. A rhyme.

Voice: 1, 2, 3, 4,

           Leila's at the kitchen door.

           5, 6, 7, 8,

           Eating apples off a plate.

- Write the rhyme on the board a line at a time and say it. Children repeat. Children say the whole rhyme.

- Teach the rhyme. Rub off the last word of each line. Children say the whole line and the missing word. Do the same with the next word. Continue until there are no words on the board. Children say the whole rhyme with no prompts.

Extension activity

Play the *I need a ... memory game* with prompts:

- Four children stand in a line or by their desks. Give each one a Flashcard to hold up. Hold one yourself.

- Prompt the first child to say, e.g. *I need a train*. Repeat the sentence and add your object, e.g. *I need a train and an orange*.

- The next child repeats your sentence and adds his/her object, e.g. *I need a train, an orange and a doll*.

- Continue until all the objects have been included. Change some or all of the Flashcards. Repeat with different children. Add more children/Flashcards into the game.

 page 58

1 Write and join

- Read the two speech bubbles to the class. Read the first one again in phrases. Children repeat. Say the whole sentence. Children repeat. Do the same with the second bubble.

- Children write over the words in each bubble. Go around checking that they are forming letters correctly.

- They join the words in the bubbles to the objects in the poster at the top of the page.

Lesson 10

Performance indicators

Children will be able to:
- sing a song
- recognise initial letter sounds aurally and write the letters
- trace eight words
- count and write numbers.

New language

The words of the song.

Review language

toys
numbers

Bring to the lesson

- the Tape
- two each of some classroom items, e.g. pens, pencils, books, rulers, etc
- the Flashcards for toys
- the word cards for *bat, teddy, doll, kite, yo-yo, ball, train, car, boat* and *bike*

PB **page 55**   WB **page 59**

Warm-up

- Practise reading all the word cards for the toys. Show the Flashcards and word cards together. Children read.
- Show the word cards only in any order. Children read.
- If your class finds it difficult, stick all the Flashcards and words together on the board and drill them thoroughly.

Presentation

- Revise plural *s*. Hold up, e.g. a pen. Ask *What is it?* Prompt *A pen/It's a pen*. Hold up two pens. Ask *How many?* Prompt *2 pens*.
- Do the same with other pairs of objects.

PB **page 55**

1 Sing

- Children look at the pictures for a minute or two. Ask them to name the toys.

- Ask *How many?* for each toy. Establish that there are two of everything.
- Point to the words of the song and read out the first line. Explain that *Hooray* is a word which children say when they are pleased about something.
- Read out the second line. Point to the first picture when you reach it and let the children say *bats*. Elicit *balls* when you come to the second picture.
- Do the same with the third line, eliciting *trains* and *planes*. Then read the fourth line.
- Play the Tape. Let children listen the first time.

Tapescript

Narrator: Topic 4. Lesson 10. Activity 1. Sing.

Children: Hooray, hooray, it's time to play!

Let's play with the bats and balls,

Let's play with the planes and trains.

It's time to play, hooray, hooray!

- Play the Tape again and encourage children to say the names of the toys as they are mentioned.

 2 Listen, say and write

- Children look at the pictures for a moment. Point to the hen and say *hen* Make sure children understand the word. Point to the pen and prompt *pen*.

- Play the Tape. Children repeat the words in the pauses then write the letter which begins each word.

Tapescript

Narrator: Topic 4. Lesson 10. Activity 2. Listen, say and write.

Voice: Hen. [pause] Hen. [pause]

Pen. [pause] Pen. [pause]

- Point again to the pictures in the book. Elicit the words. Write *hen* on the board with *pen* underneath it.

- Point to the first letter of hen and elicit /h/. Then elicit the whole word.

- Point to the first letter of pen and elicit /p/. Then elicit the whole word.

Extension activity

- Write the song from Activity 1 on the board. Add in the words represented by the pictures in the Pupil's Book.

- Teach the song. Say it a line at a time. Children repeat. Rub off the last word of each line. Children say the song filling in the missing word.

- Continue to rub off words until they can say the whole rhyme without prompts.

- Ask children to suggest other toys that could be used in the song.

- Choose four toys with simple plural endings, e.g. dolls, kites, cars and bikes (avoid teddy). Write them on the board.

- Help children say the rhyme putting in the new words.

- Children say the original rhyme and then the new one.

 page 59

1 Circle and write

- Children circle the word which correctly names the object in the picture above. They then write over the words below each picture.

Answers

cup, bat, car, tap

2 Count and write

- Children count the number of objects in each group and write the numbers in the boxes.

Answers

6, 4, 3, 9

Lesson 11 – Review

Performance indicators

Children will be able to:
- use and understand the language taught in Lessons 1–10
- write nine exemplar words.

Review language

toys
colours
Is it big/small?

Bring to the lesson

- the Tape
- the alphabet Flashcards
- the Flashcards for colours
- the word cards for *bat, teddy, doll, kite, yo-yo, ball, train, car, boat* and *bike*

PB page 56   **WB** page 60

Warm-up

- Use alphabet exemplar Flashcards to revise *a* and *an*. Show the vowel exemplar Flashcards interspersed with consonant exemplars. Elicit, e.g. *It's a goat. It's an orange*, etc.

Presentation

- Quickly practise reading the word cards for toys. Stick them on the board.

- Show the colour Flashcards. Class says the colour.

- Hold up a colour Flashcard in front of a word card. Class says, e.g. *It's a red train. It's a green bike*.

 PB page 56

1 Listen and answer

- Let children study the picture for a few moments. Prepare children for listening. Ask questions about the items in each box. Say, e.g. *Look at box number one. It's yellow. What is it?* Prompt *It's a teddy*.

- Continue with other items in both boxes.

- Play the Tape. Children answer the questions in the pauses. Stop the Tape if necessary to prompt the class to answer.

Tapescript

Narrator: Topic 4. Lesson 11. Activity 1. Listen and answer.

Adult: It's in Box 1.

Child: Is it red?

Adult: No.

Child: Is it green and white?

Adult: Yes.

Narrator: What is it? [pause]

Adult: It's in Box 2.

Child: Is it purple?

Adult: No.

Child:	Is it brown?
Adult:	Yes.
Narrator:	What is it? [pause]
Adult:	It's in Box 2.
Child:	Is it orange and white?
Adult:	Yes.
Narrator:	What is it? [pause]
Adult:	It's in Box 1.
Child:	Is it yellow?
Adult:	No.
Child:	Is it pink?
Adult:	Yes.
Narrator:	What is it? [pause]

- Play the Tape again without stopping. Children listen and answer in the pauses.

Answers

van, teddy, boat, car

2 Play the game

- Demonstrate the game. Bring a child to the front. Hold up your Pupil's Book so that you cannot see the pages but the class can. Tell the child to choose a toy and point to it. Make it clear that you cannot see which toy the child is pointing at.

- Ask questions to find out which toy it is, e.g. *Is it big? Is it red?* etc. Repeat with another child pointing to a toy and answering your questions.

- Point to a toy in your own book so that the class cannot see what it is. Say *It's a toy. What is it?* Prompt the class to ask questions to find out what it is.

- Do this again with the class in two teams taking turns to ask a question. Give a point to the team that correctly identifies the object.

- When children are confident with this activity, they can continue in pairs.

Extension activities

- Children work in pairs. They use the whole picture to point and ask questions, e.g. *What is it? What colour is it? How many … ?*

 page 60

1 Write and copy

- Children write over the alphabet exemplar words in the grid below each picture.

- They then write the words independently in the blank grids.

- Go around checking that they are forming letters correctly.

Lesson 12

Performance indicators

Children will be able to:
- use the language and handwriting skills taught in Topic 4.

Review language

Language from Topic 4

Bring to the lesson

- all the reading word cards from Topic 4
- the Flashcards for toys

 page 57   WB **page 61**

Warm-up

- Say the counting rhyme from Lesson 9, Activity 2. Children join in.
- Practise reading all the words that the class has read so far.

Presentation

- Show the Flashcards of all the toys. Class names them.

 page 57

1 Play the Flashcard game

- Play this game with the class divided into two teams.
- Hold up your book. Point out the items in the bottom row.
- Show the children the Flashcards for all the toys in the bottom row (yo-yo, car, bat, kite, teddy). Mix them up and place them face down on your desk.
- Take one of the Flashcards, e.g. the kite. Do not show it to the class. Put it aside.
- Choose a route from the top row in the Pupil's Book that will lead to the kite in the bottom row, following the arrows. For example, say *Point to the boat*. Name one of the toys arrowed below, e.g. *Point to the car*. Then name one of the toys below the car, e.g. *Point to the doll*. Do the same again, e.g. *Point to the train*.

- Hold up the Flashcard you put aside. Do not show the picture. Ask *What is it?* The teams must guess what the object is, e.g. *Is it a kite?* If they have followed the route correctly, it will be one of two possible answers (the other is the bat Flashcard). The team that guesses the answer correctly first wins a point.
- Play again, choosing a different Flashcard from the bottom row. You could also let children choose a Flashcard. Items from the bottom row can be chosen more than once, but make sure a different route down from the top row is given.

Extension activities

- Children use the pictures on page 57 to practise the language they know in pairs or small groups.

  1 Children can simply point and make statements, e.g. *It's a (red) train. It's (red). It's (big)*.

  2 Children who can use more language can give instructions and ask questions, e.g. *Find the/Point to the small train. What colour is it? What colour is the big boat? Find the yellow plane. Is it big? How many vans?* etc. (These questions can also be used with the whole class.)

page 61

- If you wish, you may use this page as a test to check on class progress in work covered in Topic 4. Give children a fixed length of time to complete each activity.

- Explain exercise 2 before you start and do an example of exercise 3 on the board so that children know what to do. You may wish to write *apple*, *bike* and *egg* on the board.

- Alternatively, you can use this page as normal Workbook exercises and explain each task in turn, keeping the whole class working together.

1 Listen and circle

- Read out the instructions to the class. Children circle the item you describe. Teacher's script: *1 Circle the small goat. 2 Circle the big car. 3 Circle the big train 4 Circle the small teddy.*

2 Circle

- Children look at each picture in turn and circle the correct word underneath.

Answers

kite, spoon, teddy, ball

3 Write *a* or *an* and complete

- Children look at each picture, say the name and then decide if they should write *a* or *an*.

- They then write over the tinted letters and write the missing words.

Answers

a ring, an apple, a bike, an egg

5 My animal pictures

In this topic pupils:

- name eight new animals (Lessons 1 and 7)
- colour from dictated instructions (Lesson 1)
- say what they can see and ask what someone else can see (Lessons 1, 2 and 8)
- match shapes and small/capital letters (Lesson 3)
- say a word's initial letter using *It begins with* … . (Lesson 4)
- read *cat, donkey, snake, camel, dog, horse, blue, green, yellow, bee, fish, frog, mouse, red, black* and *white* (Lessons 1, 2, 6, 7 and 8)

- recognise aurally, and read and write, the initial letters of consonant/vowel/consonant words *tin, bin, pot* and *cot* (Lessons 5 and 10)
- sing a new song (Lesson 10)
- agree and disagree using *True/False* (Lesson 11)
- trace and write initial letters, words and whole sentences (all Lessons)
- practise and consolidate (Lessons 6, 11 and 12)

Lesson 1

Performance indicators

Children will be able to:
- name four new animals
- say what they can see
- read *cat, donkey* and *snake*
- listen and follow instructions for colouring.

New language

camel, donkey, horse, snake
I can see … .

Reading words

cat, donkey, snake

Review language

the letters *a–z*
cat, dog

Bring to the lesson

- the Tape
- the Flashcards for cat, dog, donkey, horse, camel and snake
- word cards for *cat, donkey* and *snake*

Preparation

Use Resources page 162 to make word cards for *cat, donkey* and *snake*

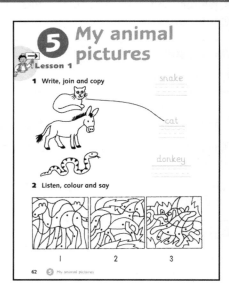

 page 58   **page 62**

Warm-up

- Write the alphabet on the board. Say the letter names as you go.

- Point to each letter. Children say the name.

- Go through the letters several times until the children can say them confidently to a steady rhythm. If you wish, clap your hands to keep a regular beat.

Presentation

- Show Flashcards to elicit *cat* and *dog*.

- Use the donkey, horse, camel and snake Flashcards to introduce the new words in the usual way.

- Put the six Flashcards around the classroom or spaced well apart on the board. Point and say e.g. *I can see a camel*. Make the meaning of *see* clear. Point to the other cards and say, e.g. *I can see a horse*, etc.

- If your class is confident point to a Flashcard and say *I can see a …* . Children say the animal you are pointing to.

 page 58

 1 Listen and find

- Children look at the pictures in their books. Tell them to listen. Play the Tape.

- As each animal is mentioned, children look for it on the page and point to it.

Tapescript

Narrator: Topic 5. My animal pictures. Lesson 1. Activity 1. Listen and find.

Child: I can see a cat, [pause] a horse, [pause] a donkey, [pause] a camel, [pause] a snake [pause] and a dog [pause].

- Play the Tape a second time. Children point to each picture and repeat the name of the animal in the pause.

2 Talk

- Point to an animal Flashcard. Say, e.g. *I can see a cat*. Children repeat. Do this again with another card.

- Point to a third Flashcard. Prompt the class to say, e.g. *I can see a donkey*.

- Point to Flashcards until the class can speak confidently.

- Say to individuals, e.g. *Karim, bring me the horse, please* until you have all the Flashcards collected together.

- Show the class a Flashcard. Prompt, e.g. *I can see a donkey*. Hold up the donkey Flashcard and one other. Say, e.g. *I can see a donkey and a cat*. Class repeats.

- Do this again, showing two different pairs of Flashcards and eliciting sentences from the class.

Reading: *cat*, *donkey* and *snake*

- Introduce the first word.

  1 Hold up the Flashcard of the cat. Class names it.

  2 Hold up the alphabet Flashcard for the letter *c*. Class says /k/.

  3 Stick the letter and picture Flashcards beside each other on the board. Point and say /c/, *cat*. Class repeats.

  4 Stick the word card for *cat* on the board. Point to it and say *cat* again. Class repeats.

  5 Hold up your book and point to the cat. Name it and point to the word below. Check children are pointing to it. Say *cat*. Class repeats. Point to the word on the board. Class reads the word.

- Introduce *donkey* and *snake* in the same way.

- Point to the words on the board in any order. Class reads.

 page 62

1 Write, join and copy

- Children write over the tinted words then match the picture to the correct word by drawing a line between them. Encourage children to draw from left to right.

- Children then copy the words in the grids.

2 Listen, colour and say

- Explain to the class that they should only colour shapes which have a dot in.

- Tell children to listen and colour. Teacher's script: Colour picture 1 brown. Colour picture 2 grey (or black). Colour picture 3 red.

- When they have finished colouring, children point and say *I can see a camel*, (*horse, dog*) etc.

Lesson 2

Performance indicators

Children will be able to:
- ask what someone can see
- read *camel*, *dog* and *horse*
- trace three new words.

New language

What can you see?

Reading words

camel, *dog*, *horse*

Review language

donkey, camel, horse, snake

Bring to the lesson

- the Tape
- the Flashcards for cat, donkey, snake, camel, dog and horse
- word cards for *cat, donkey, snake, camel, dog* and *horse*
- the alphabet Flashcards for dog, goat, lion, insect and monkey
- real classroom items: two each of pens, pencils, books, etc.

Preparation

Use Resources page 162 to make word cards for *camel, dog* and *horse*

PB page 59   WB page 63

Warm-up

- Use the Flashcards for dog, goat, lion, insect and monkey to practise *I can see a … .*
- Use Flashcards to help children play the *I can see a …* Memory chain game (see Game 15, page 9).
- Revise plural *s* using classroom items. Show one item. Class says the word. Show two of the item. Class says the word with the final *s*. Make sure they say the sound.

Presentation

- Hold up the Flashcard of one of the animals from Lesson 1. Ask *What can you see?* Elicit the answer from the whole class e.g. *I can see a dog.* Repeat with one or two other Flashcards.
- Ask individuals the question. Include the alphabet exemplars from the Warm-up.

PB page 59

1 Listen and circle

- Children look at the picture for a minute or two.
- Ask a child *What can you see?* Elicit, e.g. *I can see a camel.* Ask *How many camels?* Let the child answer if he/she can, otherwise count with the class.
- Do this again until all the animals have been identified and counted.
- Point out the small pictures below the big picture. Ask *How many … ?* for each one. Prompt *3 horses, 2 horses, 3 donkeys, 1 donkey*, etc.
- Children listen. Start the Tape. Play the question and answer for Number 1. Stop the Tape.
- Point to the big picture. Ask *How many horses?* Elicit *2 horses*. Point to the group of two horses under the big

picture and say *Circle two horses*. Demonstrate if necessary.

● Play the rest of the Tape without stopping if possible.

● Children circle the correct number of animals as it is mentioned on the Tape.

___

Tapescript

Narrator: Topic 5. Lesson 2. Activity 1. Listen and circle.

Narrator: Number 1.

Child 1: What can you see?

Child 2: I can see 2 horses. [pause]

Narrator: Number 2.

Child 2: What can you see?

Child 1: I can see 1 donkey. [pause]

Narrator: Number 3.

Child 3: What can you see?

Child 4: I can see 5 snakes. [pause]

Narrator: Number 4.

Child 4: What can you see?

Child 3: I can see 3 camels. [pause]

___

2 Talk

● Check Activity 1 with the whole class. Point to picture 1. Ask *What can you see?* Choose individuals to answer about each of the small pictures.

● Children can practise in pairs taking turns to ask the question and give the answer.

Reading: *camel, dog* and *horse*

● Introduce the first word.

1 Hold up the Flashcard of the camel. Class names it.

2 Hold up the alphabet Flashcard for the letter *c*. Class says /k/.

3 Stick the letter and picture Flashcards beside each other on the board. Point and say /k/, *camel*. Class repeats.

4 Stick the word card for camel on the board. Point to it and say *camel* again. Class repeats.

5 Hold up your book and point to the *camel* on page 58. Name it and point to the word below. Check children are pointing to it. Say *camel*. Class repeats. Point to the word on the board. Class reads the word.

● Introduce *dog* and *horse* in the same way.

● Point to the words on the board in any order. Class reads.

● Hold up word cards for all the animals the class has learned, in any order. Class reads.

 page 63

1 Trace, read and join

● Children trace round the outline animals.

● They find the correct word for each one.

● They join the word and picture with a line.

2 Count and circle. Then write, copy and say

● Children count the animals in each picture and circle the correct number on the right.

● Check answers with the whole class. Ask a child *What can you see?* Prompt, e.g. *I can see 1 camel*. (6 dogs/2 horses) Children circle the number 1 on the left.

● Children write over the tinted words in the grids.

● Children copy the words into the blank grids.

Lesson 3

Performance indicators

Children will be able to:
- recognise three commands for the care of animals
- match capital letters to small letters and write.

New language

Be careful of the donkey!
Feed the donkey.
Tie the rope.

Review language

animals

Bring to the lesson

- the Tape
- the word cards for animals
- the Flashcards for car, bike, van, cat, dog and goat
- a baby doll, or a picture of a baby, and a small spoon
- a short piece of rope and a bunch of leaves or grass

Preparation

Cut out a large picture of a car from a magazine.

PB page 60   **WB** page 64

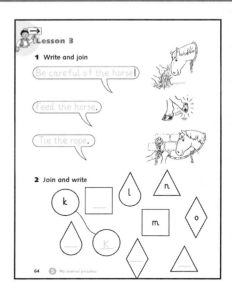

Warm-up

- Use the word cards to practise reading the words *cat, dog, camel, horse, snake* and *donkey*.

- Sing a song or play a game that the children enjoy.

Presentation

- Demonstrate the instructions taught in this Lesson. A child holds the picture of the car and stands to one side. Bring another child forward. Explain that he/she is in the road. Instruct the 'car' to drive along the road. Say to the child *Be careful of the car!* Move him/her back so the 'car' drives in front. If you wish, do this with another pair.

- Show the class the baby doll or picture. Say *The baby is crying*. Ask for suggestions of what to do. If the right answer is given say *Yes. Feed the baby*. Otherwise, give the answer yourself. Show the spoon and mime the activity, or let a child come and do it.

- Show the rope and name it. Demonstrate tying it. Say *Tie the rope*. Put animal Flashcards on the board. Hold the rope next to them. Say, e.g. *Tie the horse, Tie the camel*.

PB page 60

1 Listen and write 1, 2, 3

- Children look at the three pictures for a moment or two.

- Point to the first picture. Ask what the donkey is doing. Ask children what they should do when a donkey does this. Prompt *Be careful of the donkey!*

- Ask what the donkey is doing in the second picture. Prompt answers. Hold up the bunch of leaves and say *Feed the donkey*.

- Tell children to point to the rope. Hold up your rope, tie it and say *Tie the rope*.

- Play the Tape. Children listen and number the pictures as they hear the instruction.

Tapescript

Narrator: Topic 5. Lesson 3. Activity 1. Listen and write 1, 2 or 3

Narrator: 1.

Karim: Tie the rope.

Narrator: 2.

Samir: Feed the donkey.

Narrator: 3.

Samir: Be careful of the donkey.

Karim: Phew!

● Point to the first picture and say the instruction. Class repeats. Ask what number should be in the box (3). Do the same with the other pictures.

2 Find and say

● Children follow the jumbled strings to the correct pictures and work out and say the appropriate instruction: 1 *Feed the monkey.* 2 *Tie the rope.* 3 *Be careful of the lion.*

● Do the activity with the whole class first, then let children repeat the exercise in pairs. Go round and listen to them.

Extension activity

● Use the Flashcards for car, bike, van, cat, dog and goat. Show the car Flashcard. Prompt the class to say *Be careful of the car!* Do the same with the bike and the van Flashcards.

● Show the animal pictures in turn. Elicit *Feed the cat (dog, goat)*.

● Show the Flashcards in any order. Prompt the correct instruction for each picture.

 page 64

1 Write and join

● Children write over the tinted words.

● They join the bubbles to the correct picture.

2 Join and write

● Children draw lines between matching shapes and write the capital letter in the blank.

Lesson 4

Performance indicators

Children will be able to:
- give a word's initial letter using *It begins with … .*
- match initial letters to objects
- write single words
- fill in missing letters.

New language

It begins with … .

Review language

ball, bat, kite, dog, doll and *donkey*

Bring to the lesson

- the Tape
- the alphabet Flashcards
- the Flashcards for donkey, camel, snake, horse, cat, dog, goat, lion and monkey
- the word cards for *ball, bat, kite, dog, doll* and *donkey*

PB **page 61**   WB **page 65**

Warm-up

- Play the *Alphabet game.* Show an alphabet Flashcard. Class names it and says the initial letter sound, e.g. *Watch, /w/.*
- Only show the letter on the other side if they cannot remember the initial letter sound.

Presentation

- Hold up any one of the animal Flashcards except monkey, snake and lion. Ask *What is it?* Elicit, e.g. *It's a dog.* Say *Yes, dog. It begins with /d/.*
- Repeat with one or two other Flashcards.
- Show more Flashcards. Children name the animal. Say *It begins with … .* and prompt the class to say the initial letter sound.

PB **page 61**

🔊 1 Listen and guess

- Tell children to look at the animals and toys in the picture. Ask *What can you see?* Prompt, e.g. *I can see a lion.*
- Say *It begins with …* and prompt the class to say the initial letter sound /l/.
- Do the same with the other animals and toys in the picture.
- Tell children to listen. Play the Tape. Prompt them to name the object in the pause.

Tapescript

Narrator: Topic 5. Lesson 4. Activity 1. Listen and guess.

Child 1: It begins with /k/.

Child 2: It's a … . [pause]

Child 1: It begins with /s/.

Child 2: It's a … . [pause]

Child 1: It begins with /l/.

Child 2: It's a … . [pause]

Child 1: It begins with /v/.

Child 2: It's a … . [pause]

- Check answers with the class then play the Tape again. They answer in the pauses.

> **Answers**
>
> *car, snake, lion, van*

2 Play the game

- Hold up a Flashcard. Class names it, e.g. *Goat*. Prompt *It begins with /g/.*

- Hold up other Flashcards until the class says *It begins with …* confidently.

- Children can play the game in several ways:

  1 They work in pairs using the picture in Activity 1. Child A says *It begins with …* . Child B says *It's a …* .

  2 They work in pairs as above using any Flashcards stuck on the board.

  3 More able children work in pairs as above using animal words written on the board. Child A chooses a word and says, e.g. *It begins with /d/.* Child B reads *dog*.

Reading

- Use word cards to practise reading the words *ball, bat, kite, dog, doll* and *donkey* before children begin the Workbook exercises.

 page 65

1 Write, draw and copy

- Children write over each word, draw the correct picture in the space, then copy the words onto the grids.

2 Say, write and copy

- Children name the object then look at the word below. See if they can tell you which letter is missing. If not, write the first word on the board and ask again. Write up the other words, if necessary.

- Children write over the words and write in the missing letters.

- Children then copy the words into the grids below.

Lesson 5

Performance indicators

Children will be able to:
- recognise aurally and read the initial letters in *bin* and *tin*
- match *a* and *an* to initial consonant/vowel words
- write the missing letter in three reading words
- write words.

New language

bin, tin

Review language

a and *an*

Bring to the lesson

- the Tape
- the alphabet Flashcards for *a–g*
- 8–10 alphabet Flashcards, including some objects beginning with vowels
- the word cards for animals

PB page 62   WB page 66

Warm-up

- Use word cards to practise reading the words for animals (*cat, horse, dog, snake, camel* and *donkey*).

- Give out the alphabet Flashcards *a–g*. Children with Flashcards try to get into the correct order before the class finishes reciting the alphabet up to *g*.

Presentation

- Use the alphabet Flashcards to revise *a* and *an*. Hold up a Flashcard and ask *What is it?* Elicit *It's a/an … .*

PB page 62

1 Play the picture game

- Put several animal Flashcards on the board, spaced as far apart as possible. Include the insect Flashcard for the initial vowel sound.

- Divide the class into two teams.

- Point to all the Flashcards. Ask a child from Team A *What can you see?* Elicit, e.g. *I can see a snake.*

- Say to a child from Team B *Find the snake.* If possible, the child goes to the board and touches the correct Flashcard. Alternatively, the child stands up and points.

- Then ask a child from Team B the question. It is Team A's turn to find the animal.

2 Listen, say and write

- Children look at the pictures for a moment. Point to the tin. Say *tin*. Point to the bin. Say *bin*. Make sure children understand the words.

- Play the Tape. Children repeat in the pauses. They write the initial letter of each word.

Tapescript

Narrator: Topic 5. Lesson 5. Activity 2. Listen, say and write.

Adult: Tin. [pause] Tin. [pause]

Bin. [pause] Bin. [pause]

- Point again to the pictures in the book. Prompt the words. Write *tin* on the board with *bin* underneath it.

- Point to the first letter of *tin* and elicit /t/. Elicit the whole word.

- Point to the first letter of *bin* and elicit /b/. Elicit the whole word.

Extension activity

- Play the picture game from Activity 1 with another set of Flashcards, e.g. *toys*. The game can also be played with the Flashcards for numbers and classroom items.

 page 66

1 Say and join

- Children look at the pictures on the kites for a moment.

- Point out the words on the two hats.

- Hold up your book and point to the first picture. Ask *What is it?* Elicit *It's a monkey*.

- Continue with the other pictures eliciting *It's a/an … .* If children need the extra practice, prompt them to repeat *a* or *an* and the word once or twice.

- Children draw lines joining each picture to the correct person. Point out the example that has already been done.

2 Say, write and copy

- Children name the object then look at the word below. See if they can tell you which letter is missing. If not, write the first word on the board and ask again. Write up the other words, if necessary.

- Children write over the words and write in the missing letters.

- Children then copy the words into the grids below.

Lesson 6

Performance indicators

Children will be able to:
- read *blue*, *green* and *yellow*
- use and understand the language taught in Lessons 1–5.

Reading words

blue, green, yellow

Review language

animals

Bring to the lesson

- the Flashcards for cat, dog, goat, lion, monkey, bird, donkey, horse, camel and snake
- the Flashcards for blue, green and yellow
- word cards for *blue*, *green* and *yellow*

Preparation

Use Resources page 162 to make word cards for *blue*, *green* and *yellow*

PB **page 63**   WB **page 67**

Warm-up

- Sing the *Hooray, hooray song* (Topic 4, Lesson 10).
- Practise the *s* plural ending. Draw a simple bat on the board. Write *bat*. Draw two bats below. Write *2 bats*. Point out the plural *s*. Do the same with *ball/balls*, *train/trains* and *plane/planes*.
- Say the words of the song again. Point to the new words in the appropriate places. Children read and say them. Repeat a little faster.

Presentation

- Hold up the Flashcards for cat, dog, goat, lion, monkey, bird, donkey, horse, camel and snake. Class names them.
- Place them around the room in any order.

PB **page 63**

1 Play the Flashcard game

- Children look in their books. Point out the red and blue ticks. Tell children to look at all the pictures carefully. Give them a minute or two to look.
- Children close their books.
- Divide the class into two teams: Red and Blue. Explain that they must look at each Flashcard around the room and decide whether it had a red or blue tick in their books.
- Choose a child from each team to come to the front. Taking turns, other children tell the child at the front which Flashcards to collect for their team. The Red Team can only name animals on Flashcards with a red tick in the book. The blue team can only name animals on Flashcards with a blue tick in the book.
- Keep your own book open and check the Flashcards. If the wrong Flashcard is named, it is the other team's turn.

- Collect all the Flashcards in a pile on your desk. When you have them all, mix them up, and put them on the board in any order.

- Say to a child from the Red Team *Find a red picture*. The child must try to remember which of the pictures on the board had a red tick in the Pupil's Book

- He/She chooses a Flashcard and shows it to the rest of the Red team. Ask *Is it a red picture?* If they say *Yes* and the answer is correct, they keep it. If they say *No*, the Flashcard is put back on the board. Then it is the Blue Team's turn to take a Flashcard down.

- Choose different children to take Flashcards from the board each time. The winning team is the one which collects all the correct Flashcards first.

Extension activities

- A child from the Red Team shows one of their Flashcards to the Blue Team and asks *What can you see?* A child from the Blue team answers *I can see a ... .* Then the Blue team shows one of their Flashcards to the Red Team and asks the question.

- Continue the activity, but the team answering must say *I can see a ... . It begins with ... .*

Reading: *blue*, *green* and *yellow*

- Introduce the first word.

  1 Hold up the blue Flashcard. Class names it.

  2 Hold up the alphabet Flashcard for the letter *b*. Class says /b/.

  3 Stick the letter and picture Flashcards beside each other on the board. Point and say /b/, *blue*. Class repeats.

  4 Stick the word card for *blue* on the board. Point to it and say *blue* again. Class repeats.

- Introduce *green* and *yellow* in the same way.

- Take the word cards off the board. Hold them up in any order. Class reads.

 page 67

1 Write, find and join

- Children write over the letters of the eight words.

- They join them to the correct animal in the picture.

Lesson 7

Performance indicators

Children will be able to:
- name four new animals
- read *fish*, *mouse*, *bee* and *frog*
- trace words
- match shapes and small/capital letters.

New language

bee, fish, frog, mouse

Reading words

fish, mouse, bee, frog

Review language

toys

Bring to the lesson

- the Tape
- the word cards for toys
- the Flashcards for fish, mouse, bee and frog
- word cards for *fish, mouse, bee* and *frog*

Preparation

Use Resource page 162 to make words cards for *fish, mouse, bee* and *frog*

 page 64   **page 68**

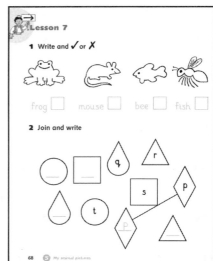

Warm-up

- Use word cards to practise reading the words for toys.

Presentation

- Use the Flashcards for fish, mouse, bee and frog to introduce the new vocabulary in the usual way.

 page 64

1 Listen, point and say

- Tell children to listen, point to each picture in turn and say the word.

- Play the first part of the Tape straight through. Prompt children to repeat in the pauses.

Tapescript

Narrator: Topic 5. Lesson 7. Activity 1. Listen, point and say.

Voice: [fish sound effect]

Fish. [pause]

[mouse sound effect]

Mouse. [pause]

[frog sound effect]

Frog. [pause]

[bee sound effect]

Bee. [pause]

- Stop the Tape and drill the words again before children hear the next part.

- Play the second part of the Tape. Children listen to the sound and decide which creature it is. They name it in the pause.

Tapescript

Narrator: Now listen again, point and say.

Voice: [mouse sound effect]

It's a … . [pause]

[frog sound effect]

It's a … . [pause]

[bee sound effect]

It's a … . [pause]

[fish sound effect]

It's a … . [pause]

- Play the whole Tape again without stopping. Children speak in the pauses.

2 Play the guessing game

- Demonstrate the game. Start to draw one of the new animals on the board. Ask *What is it?* Children guess *Is it a … ?* If they guess correctly, say *Yes* and finish the picture. If they don't, say *No*. Draw a bit more and ask again. Do this until they get the right answer.

- Do the same with the other three animals.

- If you have some confident children, let them whisper one of the animals to you before they start to draw it on the board. Tell the child when to stop drawing and ask *What is it?* Other children take turns to ask *Is it a … ?*

Alternative

- Hold up a Flashcard with a sheet of paper covering the picture.

- Lower the paper and show a bit of the picture. Ask *What is it?* and continue as above. (Use this method of playing the game for any animals or objects that are too difficult to draw.)

Extension activity

- Ask children to draw one of the new animals for homework and bring it in for the next lesson. They show the picture and ask *What is it?* Or they can show a part of it and ask the question. If children draw their own pictures, put them up on the board and around the classroom. Use them to practise *How many … ? What colour is it? Is it big/small?*

Reading: *fish, mouse, bee* and *frog*

- Introduce the first word.

1 Hold up the Flashcard of the fish. Class names it.

2 Hold up the alphabet Flashcard for the letter f. Class says /f/.

3 Stick the letter and picture Flashcards beside each other on the board. Point and say /f/, *fish*. Class repeats.

4 Stick the word card for *fish* on the board. Point to it and say *fish* again. Class repeats.

5 Hold up your book and point to the fish. Name it and point to the word below. Class repeats. Point to the word on the board. Class reads the word.

- Introduce *mouse, bee* and *frog* in the same way.

- Point to the words on the board in any order. Class reads.

 page 68

1 Write and ✓ or ✗

- Children write over the letters of each word.

- They read the word and tick the box if it matches the picture above. They put a cross if it does not.

> **Answers**
> ✓, ✓, ✗ *(fish)*, ✗ *(bee)*

2 Join and write

- Children draw lines between matching shapes and write the capital letter in the blank.

Lesson 8

Performance indicators

Children will be able to:
- ask what someone can see
- read *red, black* and *white*
- trace words for animals, singular and plural.

New language

Can you see ...?

Reading words

red, black, white

Review language

cat, dog, mouse, frog, bee, snake

Bring to the lesson

- the Tape
- the alphabet Flashcards *a–m*
- all the animal Flashcards from Topic 5
- word cards for *red, black* and *white*

Preparation

Use Resources page 162 to make word cards for *red, black* and *white*.

PB **page 65**   WB **page 69**

Warm-up

- Divide the class into two teams. Give out the alphabet Flashcards *a–m* to 13 children in Team A.
- Team B begins chanting the alphabet up to *m*. The children in Team A must stand up and hold up their Flashcard when their letter is said.
- Change over so Team A chants and Team B holds the Flashcards.

Presentation

- Show an animal Flashcard and ask a child *What can you see?* Prompt, e.g. *I can see a horse.* Ask another child, e.g. *Tony, can you see a horse?* Prompt *Yes. (I can see a horse.)* Show the Flashcard to other children and repeat the question.
- Show, e.g. the snake Flashcard and ask the whole class *Can you see a snake?* Elicit *Yes.*
- Show, e.g. the camel Flashcard and ask *Can you see a fish?* Elicit *No.*

- Do the activity again with one or two other Flashcards.

PB **page 65**

 1 Listen and say 1 or 2

- Let children look at the pictures on the mats numbered 1 and 2 for a moment.
- Say *Look at number 1. What can you see?* Prompt the class or individuals to name the four animals.
- Do the same with the second mat.
- Tell children to listen. Play the Tape. In the pauses children find the animal in the question.
- They listen to the child on the Tape saying *Yes* or *No*. They decide from the answer which mat he is looking at. They say the number in the pause.
- Stop the Tape if necessary for them to do the task.

Tapescript

Narrator: Topic 5. Lesson 8. Activity 1. Listen and say 1 or 2.

Adult: Can you see a camel?

Child 1: Yes. [pause]

Adult: Can you see a horse?

Child 2: No. [pause]

Adult: Can you see a fish?

Child 3: No. [pause]

Adult: Can you see a donkey?

Child 4: Yes. [pause]

- Play the Tape again without stopping. Children say the number of the mat in the pause.

2 Talk

- Tell children to look at the pictures on the mats in Activity 1. Ask *Can you see … ?* questions about the animals shown and the other animals the children can name that are not on the page.

- Children continue the activity in pairs or small groups. Go around listening to them. If some children find asking the question hard, pair them with more able children so that they can listen and learn how to ask it.

Extension activity

- Show animal Flashcards and demonstrate questions which include colours, e.g. *Can you see a red (green, yellow) snake?* Children answer *Yes/No*.

- Children work in pairs pointing at the mats in their books and asking similar questions. Go around listening to them.

- They can also practise *What colour is the … ?*

Reading: *red, black* and *white*

- Introduce the first word.

  1 Hold up the red Flashcard. Class names it.

  2 Hold up the alphabet Flashcard for the letter *r*. Class says /r/.

  3 Stick the letter and colour Flashcards beside each other on the board. Point and say /r/, *red*. Class repeats.

4 Stick the word card for *red* on the board. Point to it and say *red* again. Class repeats.

- Introduce *black* and *white* in the same way.

- Point to the words on the board in any order. Class reads.

 page 69

1 Find, write and join

- Children look at the animals in each picture. They write over the words below, then join each word to the correct animal in the pictures above.

- When children have finished the first task they can work in pairs taking turns to ask *Can you see a … ?* and answer *I can see a …* . Go around and listen to them.

2 Count and write

- Children count the number of animals in each group, write the number and then write over the word.

- Ask individuals to read out the answers and ask the class to repeat, checking that they clearly add the plural *s*.

Answers

2, 3, 5

Lesson 9

Performance indicators

Children will be able to:
- follow and act out a story
- complete sentences choosing from given missing words.

New language

sorry, Dad

Review language

family members
Be careful of the ... .
Feed the ... .
Tie the ... .

Bring to the lesson

- the Tape
- the Flashcards for car, bike and van
- the Flashcards for donkey, kite, fish, bee and frog
- the rope from Lesson 3
- a fresh bunch of leaves

PB **page 66**   **WB** **page 70**

Warm-up

- Use page 8 of the Pupil's Book to revise *father, mother, brother* and *sister*.

- Use the Flashcards for car, bike and van to practise *Be careful of the ... .* Show the car Flashcard. Prompt the class to say *Be careful of the car!* Write it on the board.

- Do the same with the bike and van Flashcards.

Presentation

- Show the rope. Elicit *rope*. Tie it and elicit *Tie the rope.* Remind children if they have forgotten. Write it on the board

- Hold up the Flashcard for donkey and the bunch of leaves. Prompt *Feed the donkey*.

- Remind children if they have forgotten. Write it on the board.

 PB **page 66**

 1 Listen and read

- Children look at the pictures. Ask what they think is happening.

- See if they can match any of the instructions on the board to the correct pictures.

- Play the Tape. Children listen and follow in their books.

Tapescript

Narrator: Topic 5. Lesson 9. Activity 1. Listen and read.

Father: Feed the donkey, please, Salama.

Tie the rope.

Brother: Be careful of the kite!

Sister: Be careful of the fish!

Father: Tie the rope, please, Salama.

Salama: Sorry, Dad.

- Read the speech bubbles one at a time. Class repeats.
- Play the Tape a second time for children to hear the complete story.

2 Act it out

- Divide the class into groups of four. Assign each child a part as Salama, his father, his brother or his sister. Children practise reading the dialogue. Go around listening to them.
- Play the Tape to the whole class again to help with pronunciation if necessary.
- If you have space in your classroom, children may enjoy acting this story out with all the family and a child being the donkey. One or two groups could perform it using the bunch of leaves and the rope.

Note: If children act the story, the rope should be held by the 'donkey' in his/her hand, not placed around the child's neck. Remind children that they should not put a rope around their own or anyone else's neck.

 page 70

1 Write and complete

- Children write over the four words in the boxes.
- They look at the pictures and read the speech bubbles.
- They choose the correct word from the boxes to complete each sentence and write it in the space.

Answers

Tie the rope. Feed the fish. Be careful of the bee! Be careful of the frog!

Lesson 10

Performance indicators

Children will be able to:
- Say a new rhyme
- recognise aurally and write the initial letters of *cot* and *pot*
- write the missing letter in reading words.

New language

looking at me (see song)
pot, cot

Review language

snake, fish, kite, teddy
colours

Bring to the lesson

- the Tape
- the Flashcards for animals
- the word cards for *green, yellow, blue, red, black* and *white*.

 page 67   **page 71**

Warm-up

- Play the *I need a … Memory chain game* (see Game 14, page 9).
- Use word cards to practise reading the words *green, yellow, blue, red, black* and *white*.

Presentation

- Give out several animal Flashcards. Ask, e.g. *Ali, what can you see?* The child holds up his Flashcard and says, e.g. *I can see a grey goat.*
- Ask other children the question. Children answer *I can see a … .*
- Use a Flashcard to explain *looking at me*. Hold it up in front of you and say, e.g. *I can see a brown lion looking* (point to the animal's eyes) *at me* (point to yourself). Prompt the class to repeat *looking at me*.

 page 67

1 Listen and say

- Let children look at the pictures for a few moments.
- Read out the words of the rhyme, pointing to the pictures for each verse.
- Read the verses again. Prompt children to say some of the words with you, e.g. *What can you see? I can see a … looking at me.*
- Tell children to listen. Play the Tape. Children follow in their books.

Tapescript

Narrator: Topic 5. Lesson 10. Activity 1. Listen and say.

Hassan: Mona, Mona, what can you see?

Mona: I can see a blue bird looking at me!

Hassan, Hassan, what can you see?

Hassan: I can see a monkey looking at me!

- Say the rhyme a line at a time. Children repeat. Teach the rhyme a line at a time.

- Play the Tape a second time and prompt the children to join in without looking at their books.

2 Listen, say and write

- Let children look at the pictures for a moment. Point to the pot and say *pot*. Point to the cot and say *cot*. Make sure children understand the words.

- Play the Tape. Children repeat in the pauses then write the letter which begins each word.

Tapescript

Narrator: Topic 5. Lesson 10. Activity 2. Listen, say and write.

Adult: Pot. [pause] Pot. [pause]

Cot. [pause] Cot. [pause]

- Point again to the pictures in the book. Elicit the words. Write *pot* on the board with *cot* underneath it.

- Point to the first letter of *pot* and elicit /p/. Then elicit the whole word.

- Point to the first letter of *cot* and elicit /k/. Then elicit the whole word.

Extension activity

- Give animal Flashcards to three or four confident children. They stand at the front or at their desks. Ask the first child the question as on the Tape in Activity 1, e.g. *Karim, Karim, what can you see?* Prompt the child to reply like the children on the Tape.

- Give the Flashcards to other children. Prompt the class to join you in asking the question.

- Give different animal Flashcards to different children. Class chants the question and the children show their pictures and chant the answer.

 page 71

1 Write, find and colour

- Children look at the picture. Ask *What can you see?* Write answers on the board (snake, fish, kite and teddy). Include items not hidden, e.g. tree.

- Point to the question in the speech bubble. Read it to the class or let the class read/guess what it says. Point to the other bubble. Children follow as you read. Stop before *snake*. Prompt the class to say the whole word.

- Do the same with the rest of the objects.

- Children fill in the missing letters in the words. If you wish, rub the words off the board before they do this. Alternatively, make sure all the words they need are on the board so that they can check the spelling.

- Children then write over the tinted words.

Lesson 11 – Review

Performance indicators

Children will be able to:
- agree and disagree
- use and understand the language taught in Lessons 1–10
- write nine exemplar words.

New language

true, false

Review language

Language taught in Topic 5

Bring to the lesson

- the Tape
- the Flashcards for animals
- the word cards for animals and colours

PB **page 68**   WB **page 72**

Warm-up

- Use word cards to practise reading the words for colours and animals.
- Put some colour and animal word cards together. Class reads, e.g. *green frog, white mouse, blue fish*, etc.

Presentation

- Hold up an animal Flashcard, e.g. a brown dog. Ask *What is it?* Prompt *It's a brown dog*. Say *True. It's a brown dog.*
- Now say *It's a green dog*. Shake your head and say *False. It's a brown dog.*
- Do this with a few other Flashcards. Prompt the class to respond with *True* and *False*.
- Put three or four different Flashcards on the board. Ask an individual *What can you see?* Elicit, e.g. *I can see a black horse*. Prompt the class to respond *True*.
- Say *I can see a brown horse*. Prompt the class to respond *False*.
- Do the activity again a few times using the same Flashcards.

PB **page 68**

1 Listen and say

- Tell children to look carefully at the picture for a minute or two and to find as many animals as they can.
- Ask the class *What can you see?* Encourage them to use all the words they know. If they do not say the colour ask *What colour is the … ?* Ask *How many … ?*
- Tell children to listen. Play the Tape. Children respond *True/False* according to whether they think the statement is correct or not.
- If children give different answers, or no answer at all, you may need to stop the Tape for them to check the picture.

Tapescript

Narrator: Topic 5. Lesson 11. Activity 1. Listen and say.

Voice: I can see a yellow bird. [pause]

I can see three horses. [pause]

I can see four bees. [pause]

I can see a grey donkey. [pause]

I can see a blue and yellow snake. [pause]

- Children check the picture. Play the Tape again. Children reply in the pause.

2 Play the game

- Play this game with the picture in Activity 1 with the whole class at first.

- Ask questions which prompt the answer *No*, e.g. *Can you see a black bird? Can you see four camels?* Children reply with the correct details, e.g. *No. I can see a yellow bird. No. I can see one camel.*

- When children are confident with answering questions that require a negative answer they can work in pairs or small groups. Go around listening to them. Help them to ask questions that require a negative answer.

- If some children find the activity difficult, they can make statements or ask questions which require a positive answer.

Extension activity

- Practise reading all the words for the animals in the picture on page 68 (*camel, snake, horse, donkey, bee, bird*). Stick the word cards on the board in any order.

- Divide the class into two teams. Show a Flashcard, e.g. a camel, to a child from Team A, who says *I can see a camel*.

- A child from Team B must find the word on the board. If he/she can do it, Team B gets a point. If not, a child from Team A can find it for a point.

- The child who gets it right puts the Flashcard up next to the word card.

 page 72

1 Write and copy

- Children write over the alphabet exemplar words in the grid below each picture. Go around checking that they are forming letters correctly.

- Children then copy the words into the blank grids below.

Lesson 12

Performance indicators

Children will be able to:
- use the structure a + *(colour)* + *(noun)*
- use and understand the language taught in Topic 5.

Review Language

colours
objects

Bring to the lesson

- the Flashcards for colours
- the word cards for colours
- different coloured objects
- the Flashcards and word cards from Topics 4 and 5
- word cards for *pen, pencil, horse, ball, bag* and *cat*
- six word cards for *a*

Preparation

Use Resources page 162 to make six word cards for *a* and one each for *pen, pencil, horse, bag* and *cat*. (You already have a wordcard for *ball*.)

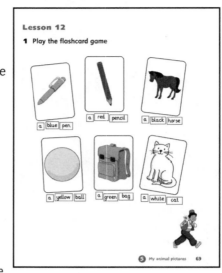

[PB] **page 69**   [WB] **page 73**

Warm-up

- Say the rhyme from Lesson 10.
- Put the colour Flashcards in any order on the board. Put the matching word cards in two piles on your desk. Children take turns in teams to come out, pick a word card from their pile and stick it under the correct Flashcard.
- Class reads the words.

Presentation

- Hold up an object. Ask *What is it?* Elicit, e.g. *It's a (yellow) pencil.* (If the colour is not given in the answer, ask *What colour is it?*)
- Ask about another object. Prompt children to include the colour in the answer.
- Do the same with several other objects.

[PB] **page 69**

1 Play the Flashcard game

- Put the Flashcards for pen, pencil, horse, ball, bag and cat face up on your desk.
- Children open their books and look at the pictures and captions. See if they can read what they say. If they can do this, put the word cards to make up the same phrases on the board. Children read again.
- If they have difficulty, point and ask *What is it?* Elicit, e.g. *It's a pen.* Put the word card for pen on the board. Ask *What colour is it?* Class answers *It's blue.* Hold up the *blue* word card. Class reads. Put it on the board. Add the word card for *a* and help children to read the whole caption.
- Do the same with the other captions, as necessary.

- Choose a child to find the correct Flashcard from your desk and stick it above the caption on the board. Do the same with the other Flashcards and captions.

Extension activity

- Play a *Caption/Flashcard matching game*.

- Put all the colour and object word cards on your desk. Put the *a* word cards on the board.

- Divide the class into two teams. Two children from Team A put up a colour word card and an object word card on the board with an indefinite article. If Team B can read it, they get a point. Then it is their turn to choose and Team A must read.

 page 73

- If you wish, you may use this page as a test to check on class progress in work covered in Topic 5. Give children a fixed length of time to complete each activity.

- Explain the exercises before you start so that children know what to do. You may wish to write *rope* on the board.

- Alternatively, you can use this page as normal Workbook exercises and explain each task in turn, keeping the whole class working together.

1 Circle

- Children read the words and circle the one which matches the picture above.

> **Answers**
> *donkey, camel, mouse, bag, frog, snake*

2 Write and complete

- Children look at the pictures and complete the instructions below.

> **Answers**
> *Feed the donkey! Tie the rope.*

3 Read, colour and write

- Children read the tinted colour words, colour the pictures appropriately and then write over the words.

6 My fun games

In this topic pupils:

- name, read and write *run, hop, skip* and *jump* (Lessons 1, 2, 4 and 12)
- say actions they/other children can/can't do, and instruct actions (Lessons 1, 2, 4)
- read and write *I can/can't; count to 10, ride a bike, whistle, swim; Can you; Yes, No* (Lessons 1, 2, 4, 7 and 12)
- compose simple sentences using word cards (Lessons 1 and 6)
- read/trace/complete sentences, questions and phrases (all Lessons)
- understand colours of traffic lights and road safety instructions (Lesson 3)

- describe an animal (Lesson 5)
- talk about what is in a picture (Lessons 5 and 8)
- recognise aurally and write initial letters for c/v/c words (Lessons 5 and 10)
- match shapes and write corresponding capital letters (Lesson 5)
- read *pink, purple, orange, brown* and *grey* (Lessons 6 and 8)
- ask about ability (Lesson 7)
- read and act out a simple story (Lesson 9)
- sing and learn a song (Lessons 10 and 12)

Lesson 1

Performance indicators

Children will be able to:
- name four actions
- say what actions they can do
- read *I can*
- read and write *run, hop, skip* and *jump*.

New language

run, hop, jump, skip
I can ... .

Reading words

I can, run, hop, skip, jump

Review language

Greetings
animals, colours and numbers
big, small

Bring to the lesson

- the Tape
- the Flashcards for run, hop, jump and skip
- word cards for *I can* and *run, hop, jump* and *skip*

Preparation

Use Resources page 162 to make word cards for *I can* and *run, hop, jump* and *skip*.
(Optional) Make four or five sets of word cards for *I can* and *run, hop, jump* and *skip* (see Extension Activities).

 page 70

 page 74

Warm-up

● Sing *Hello and good morning* from Topic 1, Lesson 10.

Presentation

● Use the Flashcards for *run, hop, jump* and *skip* to introduce the new vocabulary in the usual way (see Topic 1, Lesson 1, Introducing new words).

> **Note:** Make sure children understand the difference between hop and skip:
>
> hop – jump up and down on the same leg
>
> skip – a forward hop on one leg, then a forward hop on the other leg.

page 70

1 Listen and find

● Children look at the pictures. Point to each picture. Children name the action.

● Tell the class to listen. Play the Tape. Children look at the four pictures as they listen. They point to the correct action in the pauses.

Tapescript

Narrator: Topic 6. My fun games. Lesson 1. Activity 1. Listen and find.

Samir: I can jump.

Boy: Well done! [pause]

Rania: I can skip. [pause]

Leila: I can run. [pause]

Karim: I can hop, hop, hop. [pause]

---

2 Say and do

● Put the action Flashcards on the board and point to them one at a time. Prompt the class to say sentences, e.g. *I can run, I can hop*, etc. Continue until the class speaks confidently.

● Bring four children to the front. Give them an action Flashcard each. They show it to the class, say *I can …* and do the action. Class repeats the sentence.

● Do this again with another four children.

● Divide the class into four teams. In turns, show each team a Flashcard. The team says the sentence and does the action. Continue until each team has had a chance to do at least two or three of the actions.

> **Note:** If you have space outside, take the children out. Tell each team to make a circle. They do the actions going round in a circle. If you stay in the classroom, show the class how to do the actions moving on the spot.

Reading: *run, hop, jump, skip* and *I can*

● Introduce the reading words in the usual way (see Topic 4, Lesson 1, Reading).

● Make sentences with two of the word cards, e.g. *I can run*. Say the sentence. Class repeats.

● Hold up the *I can* word card with the other action word cards. Class reads the sentences.

Extension activities

● Put the word cards for *run, hop, jump, skip* and *I can* on your desk. Children take turns to hold up cards to make sentences. Class reads.

Alternatively:

● Play this as a team game. One team holds up word cards for the other team to read.

● Divide the class into four or five groups and give them each a complete set of the word cards you have made (*I can* and *run, hop, jump* and *skip*). Children make sentences and read them around the group. Go around listening to some of them reading.

page 74

1 Write, join and complete

● Children write over the words in the boxes.

● Children look at the actions shown in the pictures.

● They join the words in the boxes with the correct actions.

● They write over the tinted words and write the correct word from the boxes above in each blank to complete the sentences in the speech bubbles.

● Check answers by asking children to read out each sentence. Write them on the board. The whole class reads. Children read and check their own answers.

Lesson 2

Performance indicators

Children will be able to:
- say what other children can do
- give instructions to do actions
- write short sentences and descriptive phrases.

New language

Karim/Samir/Rania/Leila can ... .

Review language

I can jump/hop/skip/run.

Bring to the lesson

- the Tape
- the alphabet flashcards for n–z
- word cards for *I can* (x4), *jump, hop, skip* and *run*
- the Flashcards for jump, hop, skip and run
- the Flashcards for Karim, Samir, Rania and Leila

Preparation

If you didn't make extra sets for the Extension activity in Lesson 1, make three more *I can* word cards so that – along with the one you prepared in Lesson 1 – you have four in total.

 PB **page 71**   **WB** **page 75**

Warm-up

- Say the *I can see* rhyme from Topic 5, Lesson 10.

- Divide the class into two teams. Give out alphabet Flashcards *n–z* to 13 children in Team A.

- Team B begins chanting the alphabet from *n*. The children in Team A must stand up and hold up their Flashcard when their letter is said.

- Change over so Team A chants and Team B holds the Flashcards.

Presentation

- Divide the class into two teams. Put the word cards for *I can* (x4) and for *jump, hop, skip* and *run* on the board. Put the Flashcards for jump, hop, skip and run face down on your desk.

- A child from Team A chooses a Flashcard and shows it to the whole class. Team A says, e.g. *I can jump*.

- A child from Team B finds the matching word card and an *I can* word card on the board and puts them together. Team B reads the sentence. Then it is their turn to choose a Flashcard.

- When the four sentences are on the board, the whole class reads.

 PB **page 71**

1 Listen and number

- Children look at the pictures of the course characters doing different actions. Hold up your book and point to each of the pictures in turn and elicit *jump, run, skip* and *hop*.

- Tell children to listen. Play the Tape. They listen to the number then to the character doing the action. They write the number under the correct picture. If your class finds this difficult, let them listen and point to the picture the first time. Then play the Tape again. They write the number in the pause.

Tapescript

Narrator: Topic 6. Lesson 2. Activity 1. Listen and number.

Adult: Number 1.

Leila: I can skip. [pause]

Adult: Number 2

Karim: I can jump. [pause]

Adult: Number 3.

Rania: I can hop. [pause]

Adult: Number 4

Samir: I can run. [pause]

- Point to the pictures in turn. Say, e.g. *Look. Karim can jump.* Class repeats. Do the same with *Samir can run. Leila can skip. Rania can hop.*

- Hold up a character Flashcard and an action Flashcard together. Elicit the correct sentence, e.g. *Leila can run.* Do the same with other pairs of Flashcards.

2 Play the game

This game can be played in a number of ways:

- Instruct the class yourself, e.g. *Jump, Run,* etc. Children do the actions at their desks.

- Bring one or two children forward to give instructions to the rest of the class.

- Put the action Flashcards face down on your desk. Bring a child forward to choose a Flashcard and instruct the class.

- Put the word cards for *run, jump, hop* and *skip* face down. A child chooses a word card, reads the word and instructs the rest of the class. The child holds the word card up and the children say the word as they do the action.

Extension activities

Whole class action games:

- Give instructions, e.g. *Jump, Hop, Skip, Run, Stand up, Sit down,* etc. Last one to do it is out.

- Give instructions as above. Include *Stop*. The last one to stop moving is out.

 page 75

1 Write and ✓

- Children write over the words in the speech bubbles. They tick the action word which fits the picture. As they work, go around checking correct formation of letters.

- To check answers, ask children to read out each speech bubble. Write answers on the board. Children read and check their answers.

2 Write and colour

- Children write over the words under each picture and colour them accordingly.

Lesson 3

Performance indicators

Children will be able to:
- understand the meaning of traffic light colours
- understand instructions for crossing a road safely
- read words for crossing a road safely

New language

bus, look left, look right, wait

Review language

stop, go

Bring to the lesson

- the Tape
- picture cards with red/green circles (see Topic 2, Lesson 10)
- a picture card with an orange circle

Preparation

- On a piece of paper or card draw and colour a large orange circle (see Warm-up).
- Make signs with arrows pointing left and right for *Look left/right*.
- (Optional) Make word cards for *Stop, Go, Wait, Look left* and *Look right* (see Play the game).

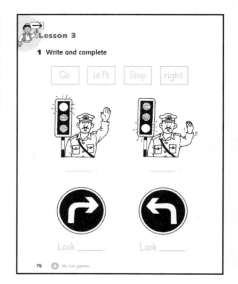

PB **page 72**   WB **page 76**

Warm-up

- Play the *Stop and go game* in teams (see Game 11, page 9). Give each team an animal name.

Presentation

- Write *left* on the left of the board and *right* on the right. Point and say the words. Children repeat.
- Point to the children's right and say *Point to the right*. Children point right. Do the same with *left*.
- Say *Look right*. Turn your head to the children's right. Write *Look right* on the board. Children read. Do the same with *left*.
- Give the four instructions (*Stop, Go, Look left, Look right*) in random order a few times.
- Show the red circle and prompt the class to say *Stop*. Show the green circle and elicit *Go*.

- Show the orange circle and say *Wait*. Class repeats. Explain it, if necessary.
- Put the three circles on the board and write the words underneath. Children read.
- Hold up your book, point to the bus and say *bus*. Children repeat. Write it on the board. Children read.

PB **page 72**

🔊 1 Listen and ✓

- Let children look at the two sequences of pictures for a moment. Hold up your book and point to the first picture in the first sequence. Ask children to say what it means: *Stop*.

- Continue with the other pictures. Do the same with the second sequence.

- Tell children they will hear Karim and Samir talking in the street. Samir is telling Karim how to cross the road safely. The conversation will match one of the sequences in their book. They must listen and match what they hear to one of the sequences.

- Play the Tape. Children listen and look at the picture sequences. Do not let them tick the box yet.

Tapescript

Narrator: Topic 6. Lesson 3. Activity 1. Listen and tick.

Samir: Stop! [pause] Wait!

Karim: Yes.

Samir: Look left.

Karim: Mm!

Samir: Look right.

Karim: Yes. [pause] Go?

Samir: No. Be careful of the bus.

Karim: Sorry.

Samir: Now go!

Karim: Go?

Samir: Yes! Go!

- Play the Tape again. Children listen then tick the box.

Answers
Box 2

2 Play the game

- Bring five children to the front to hold the coloured circles and the direction signs. If you wish, stick word cards under the circles/arrows (*Stop, Go, Wait, Look left and Look right*). Children hold up the signs in turn. Class says/reads the instruction.

- Explain that children must sit down for *Stop*, stand still for *Wait* and walk on the spot for *Go*. Practise these instructions. Practise *look left* and *look right*.

- Start the game. Give the instructions slowly at first. Children at the front hold up the correct signs and the class does the action. Gradually speed up. Change over the children holding the signs once or twice.

Extension activity

- Put the signs on the board. Start the activity with the children all standing up in the wait position.

- Point to a card. Class reads the instruction and then does the action, as in the game.

 page 76

1 Write and complete

- Children write over the words in the boxes.

- They then complete the sentences by writing over the tinted words and writing the correct words from the boxes in the spaces.

Lesson 4

Performance indicators

Children will be able to:

● say which actions they can't do
● say which actions other children can't do
● read *can't* and short sentences
● complete a sentence with a missing word
● write a short sentence.

New language

I can't ... .
Karim/Samir/Leila/Rania can't ... .

Reading words

I can't

Review language

hop, jump, run, skip

Bring to the lesson

● the Tape
● the Flashcards for animals
● the Flashcards for hop, jump, run and skip
● word cards for *I can't* and *hop, jump, run* and *skip*

Preparation

Use Resources page 162 to make a word card for *I can't.*

PB **page 73**   WB **page 77**

Warm-up

● Play the *I can see a ... Memory chain game* (see Game 15, page 9), saying animals going round the class.

● Put animal Flashcards up as prompts if necessary. When children are practised at this game they should be able to think of animals without prompts.

Presentation

● Use the action Flashcards to introduce *I can't ... .* Put the Flashcards on the board, point to one and say, e.g. *I can jump.* Draw a tick underneath.

● Point to another, shake your head and say, e.g. *I can't run.* Draw a cross underneath.

● If you wish, demonstrate *can* and *can't* clearly by repeating the sentences and doing or nor being able to do the actions. Alternatively, repeat the sentences using expressions and gestures to make the meaning clear.

● Point to the Flashcards and prompt the class to repeat each sentence.

● Do this again with *hop* and *skip*.

PB **page 73**

▭ 1 Listen and point

● Children look at the pictures that the course characters are holding. Give them time to look at each action and the cross or tick below.

● Tell the class to listen. Play the Tape. Children listen to each statement and point to the picture of the course character who is speaking. Check to see that children are pointing correctly.

Narrator: Topic 6. Lesson 4. Activity 1. Listen and point.

Samir: I can run and jump. I can't skip. [pause]

Karim: I can hop. I can't skip. [pause]

Leila: I can't skip and I can't hop. [pause]

Rania: I can hop and skip. [pause]

- Play the Tape a second time. Children listen and point.

- Point to each of the characters and elicit sentences, eg. *Samir can't skip*, etc.

2 Look and circle

- Children look at the drawings. Hold up your book and point to each one in turn and elicit the word, e.g. *hop*, etc.

- Point to the first cross and say/prompt *can't*. Point to the first tick and say/prompt *can*.

- Point to the first picture. Say *I can hop*. Circle the tick. Demonstrate circling the tick. Do the same with *I can't hop* and the cross. Tell the class to look at the pictures and circle the tick or cross.

- Children circle to make their own statements. Check understanding as they work. Point to a picture with a circled tick/cross and prompt the correct sentence.

- When the class has finished the task they work in pairs or small groups and tell each other what they can and can't do. Ask individuals to tell the class.

Reading: *I can't*

- Hold up the word card for *I can't*. Say the phrase. Class repeats. Hold an action word card alongside the *I can't* word card, e.g. *run*. Say the complete sentence, e.g. *I can't run*. Class repeats.

- Repeat step 1 with another action card.

- Hold up *I can't* and a third action card. Prompt the class to read the sentence. Practise if necessary. Do the same with the last action card.

 page 77

1 Write and complete

- Children look at the cards held by the child characters. They decide what each one is saying.

- They write over the words in the first bubble and write in the correct action to complete the sentence. Repeat for the second bubble.

- Children then write complete sentences in the remaining two bubbles.

Lesson 5

Performance indicators

Children will be able to:
- describe an animal
- recognise aurally and write initial letters for consonant/vowel/consonant words *rug* and *mug*
- write a descriptive phrase
- match shapes and write corresponding capital letters.

New language

Reading: *It's a + (colour) + (noun)*.

Review language

It begins with ... .
toys and animals

Bring to the lesson

- the Tape
- the Flashcards for animals and toys
- the word cards for animals and toys
- word cards for *It's* and *a*

Preparation

Use Resources page 162 to make a word card for *It's*. You should still have an *a* word card from Topic 5, Lesson 12.

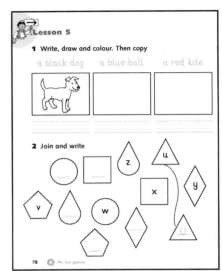

PB **page 74**   WB **page 78**

Warm-up

- Use word cards to practise reading all the animal and toy words. Use Flashcards to help word recognition if necessary.

Presentation

- Quickly show the animal Flashcards one by one. Class says the words.
- Show, e.g. the camel and ask *Is it small?* Elicit *No, it's big.*
- Ask *What colour is it?* Elicit *It's brown.* Say *It begins with ... .* Elicit /k/. Repeat the description. *It's big. It's brown. It begins with /k/.*
- Show another Flashcard and ask questions about size and colour. Elicit the initial letter.
- Select a Flashcard but do not show the class. Describe the animal as above. Ask *What is it?* See if the children can guess the answer.

PB **page 74**

1 Play the game

- Divide the class into two teams. Choose a Flashcard and describe the animal. Ask *What is it?* The first team to answer correctly wins a point.
- Do this with several Flashcards.
- Teach the class how to make up a description. Show a Flashcard. Describe it sentence by sentence, e.g. *It's big. It's black. It begins with /h/.* Class repeats each sentence. Begin the last sentence. Class says the answer, e.g. *It's a ... horse.*
- Choose other Flashcards to describe to the teams. Class repeats the description and adds the answer.
- Confident children can choose a Flashcard and describe it for the other team to guess. Give help as necessary.

Then the whole class repeats the description and adds the answer.

- When all the Flashcards have been shown, hold them up in any order and prompt the class to give the whole description, e.g. *It's small. It's green. It begins with /f/. It's a frog.*

Reading: *It's a + (noun)*

- Use the *It's* and the *a* word cards to teach the class to read *It's a + (noun)*. Use the same method as for *I can't* (see Lesson 4, Reading). Practise with the animal word cards. Children read, e.g. *It's a frog,* etc.

Extension activities

- Play the describing game with the set of toy Flashcards.

- Alternatively, show the class some real classroom objects. Put them in a box. Give the description in the usual way. The class must decide which object in the box is being described.

- If you made any sets of small cards for classroom objects in Topic 1, children can play this game in small groups or pairs.

2 Listen, say and write

- Children look at the pictures for a moment. Point to the rug and say *rug*. Point to the mug and say *mug*. Make sure children understand the words.

- Play the Tape. Children repeat in the pauses then write the letter which begins each word.

Tapescript

Narrator: Topic 6. Lesson 5. Activity 2. Listen, say and write.

Adult: Rug. [pause] Rug. [pause]

Mug. [pause] Mug. [pause]

- Point again to the pictures in the book. Elicit the words. Write *rug* on the board with *mug* underneath it.

- Point to the first letter of *rug* and elicit /r/. Then elicit the whole word.

- Point to the first letter of *mug* and elicit /m/. Then elicit the whole word.

 page 78

1 Write, draw and colour. Then copy

- Children write over the phrases and copy them into the grids below. They draw and colour the items to match each phrase.

2 Join and write

- Children draw lines between matching shapes and write the capital letter in the blank.

Lesson 6

Performance indicators

Children will be able to:
- compose simple sentences using word cards
- read *pink*, *purple* and *orange*
- write descriptive phrases.

New language

four red birds

Reading words

pink, purple, orange

Review language

colours, toys, animals and numbers

Bring to the lesson

- the Flashcard and word cards for snake, car, bike, monkey, balloon, mouse, green, yellow, blue, black, red and white
- word cards for *It's* (x6) and *a* (x6)
- four or five sets of word cards. Each set should contain It's (x6), a (x6), snake, car, bike, monkey, balloon, mouse, green, yellow, blue, black, red and white
- word cards for *pink, purple* and *orange*

Preparation

- Use Resources page 162 to make up to 6 word cards for *It's* and *a*
- Use Resources page 162 to make word cards for *pink, purple* and *orange*
- Use Resources page 162 to make four or five sets of word cards for group work. Each set should include *It's* (x6), *a* (x6), snake, car, bike, money, balloon, mouse, green, yellow, blue, black and white

 PB **page 75**   WB **page 79**

Warm-up

- Revise reading words for toys, animals and colours.
- Stick the 6 Flashcards of toys and animals on the board. Place the matching word cards on your desk. Ask a child to name a toy or animal. Another child finds the word card and sticks it next to the Flashcard.

Presentation

- Hold up word cards *It's* and *a*. Hold them next to a word from the board. Children read, e.g. *It's a bike*. Put the word card *bike* face up on your desk.
- Continue with the other words until all the word cards are removed from the board.

PB **page 75**

1 Play the Flashcard game

- Children look at the picture for a moment. While they do this, take the 6 Flashcards off the board and place them face down in a pile next to the word cards.
- Ask a child to come and turn over a Flashcard and stick it on the board. Ask *What is it?* Class replies, e.g. *It's a monkey*.
- Another child finds the word card for *monkey* and sticks it under the picture.
- A third child finds the other parts of the sentence (*It's* and *a*) and puts them on the board. Class reads the whole sentence, e.g. *It's a monkey*.

- Do the same with the other Flashcards and word cards.
- Hold up a colour Flashcard that matches a picture card. Class reads.
- Point to the picture and ask *What is it?* Prompt, e.g. *It's a black monkey.*
- Put the colour word card in the right place in the sentence. Class reads the whole sentence.
- Repeat with the rest of the other Flashcards.

Reading: *pink, purple* and *orange*

- Introduce the colour words cards in the usual way (see Topic 5, Lesson 6, Reading).

Extension activities

- Play the Flashcard game in two teams with colours. Put the 6 Flashcards on the board. Put all the colour word cards in a pile on your desk. Lay the object word cards face up on your desk and the *It's* and *a* word cards in two piles.
- A child from Team A chooses a colour word and puts it under a Flashcard it matches.
- A child from Team B takes an *It's* and an *a* word card and finds the correct word card to make a sentence describing the Flashcard.
- Team A must then read the whole sentence.
- If the teams can do the tasks, they get a point each. If they make a mistake the other team can try to correct it.
- Use small sets of word cards. Children work in four or five groups and put together the six sentences that match the objects on the board. You could do this without the colours first, then add them in.

 page 79

1 Colour, count and write

- Children decide what colour to use for each of the different birds in the picture. Explain that they must colour all the birds of one type in the same colour.
- They count the number of birds of each type, write the number and the colour, then write over *birds*. Go around checking their work.
- When they have finished, ask individuals to stand up and read out one of the phrases they have written. Check for clear pronunciation of the plural *s*.

Lesson 7

Performance indicators

Children will be able to:
- ask about ability
- name four new actions
- read *count to 10, ride a bike, whistle, swim, Yes, No* and *Can you*
- read short questions
- write words for actions, *Yes* and *No*.

New language

Can you ... ?

Reading words

count to 10, ride a bike, whistle, swim, Yes, No, can you

Review language

I can ... .

Bring to the lesson

- the Tape
- the Flashcards for count to 10, ride a bike, whistle and swim
- the word cards for *I can* and *hop, jump, run* and *skip*
- word cards for *count to 10, ride a bike, whistle, swim, Yes, No, Can you* and *?*
- tick and cross cards

Preparation

- Make large cards, one with a tick and one with a cross (see Activity 2).
- Use Resources page 162 to make word cards for *count to 10, ride a bike, whistle, swim, Yes, No, Can you* and *?*

PB **page 76** WB **page 80**

Warm-up

- Revise reading *I can run/jump*, etc. Hold up word cards. Class reads and does the action.

Presentation

- Say *I can jump*. Ask a child, e.g. *Ali, can you jump?* Prompt *Yes, I can*. The child jumps on the spot. Do the same with *hop/run/skip* and other children.

- Ask two others *Can you ... ?* Prompt *Yes, I can*.

- Show the Flashcard for *count to ten*. Point and say *1, 2, 3. I can count: 1, 2, 3*. Ask the class *Can you count?* Prompt the class to count with you. Say *I can count*. Class repeats.

- Ask *Can you count to 10?* Class counts. Say *I can count to 10*. Class repeats.

- Show the boy riding a bike. Point to the bike. Ask *What is it?* Elicit *It's a bike*. Say *I can ride a bike*. Ask the class *Can you ride a bike?* Elicit *Yes/No* answers. Say *I can ride a bike* or *I can't ride a bike* as appropriate. Class repeats.

- Do the same with the Flashcards for whistle and swim. Prompt answers *Yes/No, I can/can't*. Model the answers if necessary. Class repeats.

page 76

1 Listen and point

- Children look at the pictures. Say *Look at Rania. Rania can count to ten*. Read out the speech bubble. Ask *Can you count to 10?* Prompt answers. Let a child count to ten.

- Point to the second picture. Say *Look. Leila can't ride a bike.*

- Point to the other two pictures. Prompt *Samir can't whistle. Karim can swim.*

- Play the Tape. Children listen and point to the correct picture in the pause.

Tapescript

Narrator: Topic 6. Lesson 7. Activity 1. Listen and point.

Salama: Can you count to 10?

Rania: Yes, I can. 1, 2, 3, 4, 5, 6, 7, 8, 9, 10. [pause]

Salama: Can you ride a bike?

Leila: Er … no, I can't. [pause]

Salama: Oops! Can you whistle?

Samir: Er … no, I can't. [pause]

Salama: Can you swim?

Karim: Yes, I can.

Salama: That's good!

2 Talk

- Show the new action Flashcards one at a time. Ask *Can you … ?* questions. Help children form answers.

- Divide the class into two teams. Put the Flashcards face down on your desk. Give the tick and cross cards to a child in Team B.

- A child from Team A chooses a Flashcard and shows it to the class. Team A asks, e.g. *Can you swim?* Help if necessary.

- The Team B child holds up the tick or cross. Team B answers *Yes/No, I can/can't.*

- Continue with the teams taking turns to show Flashcards, ask and answer.

- In pairs, children take turns to point to pictures in Activity 1 and ask questions.

- If children need more practice in forming the question, they can look back at the pictures on pages 70 to 71 of the Pupil's Book and ask *Can you jump?* etc.

Reading: *count to 10, ride a bike, whistle, swim, Yes, No and Can you*

- Introduce the first phrase:

  1 Stick up the Flashcard picture of the girl counting. Prompt *Count to 10*.

  2 Stick up the word card on the board. Point and say *Count to 10*. Class repeats.

  3 Hold up your book and point to the first picture in Activity 1. Point to the words below. Check children are pointing. Say *Count to 10*. Class repeats. Point to the word card on the board. Class reads.

- Introduce the other phrases and words in the same way.

- Point to the phrases/words on the board in any order. Class reads. When teaching *Can you* with whole sentences, remember to use the *?* word card at the end.

- Take the word cards off the board. Hold them up in any order. Class reads.

 page 80

1 Write and join

- Children read and write over the words in the centre and join them to the correct pictures on either side.

2 Write and say

- Children read the question in the first speech bubble. They write over the answers in the small bubbles.

- Children practise in pairs, asking the question and answering *Yes/No, I can/can't*. Children who find this hard just say *Yes/No*.

- Repeat for the question in the second speech bubble. Children write the sentences.

Lesson 8

Performance indicators

Children will be able to:
- talk about a picture
- read *brown* and *grey*
- write sentences
- write about objects they can see in a picture.

Reading words

brown, grey

Review language

true, false

Bring to the lesson

- word cards for transport, toys, animals and colours
- 6 or 7 Flashcards of animals and transport
- the Flashcards for brown and grey
- word cards for *brown* and *grey*

Preparation

Use Resources page 162 to make word cards for *brown* and *grey*.

 PB **page 77**   **WB** **page 81**

Warm-up

- Use word cards to practise all the reading words for transport, toys, animals and the colours the children have learned so far. Leave them on the board in their groups.

Presentation

- Hold up the animal and transport Flashcards one by one. Ask individuals *Can you see a … ?* Elicit *Yes/No, I can/can't see a … .*
- Add colour into the question, e.g. *Can you see a yellow car?*

PB **page 77**

1 Talk about the picture

Note: Children can prepare for this activity by looking and talking in pairs first. Alternatively, individuals tell you what they can see straight away.

- Tell children to look for the transport items first. Then ask them to find the animals. Finally they look for the toys.
- If children work in pairs, go around listening to them. Encourage them to describe objects using colour, e.g. *I can see a red car.*
- If children do not work in pairs, give them a few minutes to look at the picture before asking the class *What can you see?*

- When individuals say what they can see, check that all children have found the item. Ask, e.g. *Fatima, can you see a ball?* Elicit *Yes, I can see a ball.* Check by asking the child to point, or ask additional questions, e.g. *What colour is the ball? Is it big/small?*

2 Play the game

- This game can be played in pairs. Children say what they can see in the picture in Activity 1 and their partners agree or disagree using *True* and *False*. Go around listening to the pairs.

- Make sure children understand that they can make false statements. Demonstrate with a child in front of the class before children work in pairs.

- Alternatively, do it as a class activity and bring students forward to make statements. Choose other children to say *True* or *False*.

- Encourage children to talk about size and colour, e.g. *I can see a red bike. I can see a small boat.*

Play the game in teams

The activity can also be made into one of these team games:

1 ● A child from Team A points to a word card on the board and reads it.

  ● If he/she does this correctly he/she shows it to the rest of Team A.

  ● They read it and say, e.g. *I can see a donkey*.

  ● Team B says *True* or *False* depending on whether they think the animal/object is in the picture or not.

  ● Give points for correct reading and a correct True/False response from the other team.

2 ● Ask Team A *What can you see?* Choose an individual to say any statement about the picture, e.g. *I can see a black cat.*

  ● Give a point for a correctly structured statement, then it is Team B's turn.

  ● The winning side is the one which can make the most correct statements.

  ● Variation: Ask children *What can't you see?* Children make correct statements, e.g. *I can't see a lion.*

Reading: *brown* and *grey*

- Introduce the colour reading words in the usual way (see Topic 5, Lesson 6, Reading).

page 81

1 Find, circle and write

- Children look at the pictures and read the words below each one.

- They circle the words according to what is in each picture.

- They read and write over the beginning of the sentence in the first speech bubble.

- They copy into the space the first word they circled below the picture.

- They read and write over the rest of the sentence.

- They write the other two words in the gaps.

- Repeat for the second speech bubble.

> **Answers**
>
> *Picture 1 (boy): I can see a car, a boat and a bike.*
> *Picture 2 (girl): I can see a donkey, a fish and a train.*

Lesson 9

Performance indicators

Children will be able to:
- read and act out a story
- write and complete sentences with a missing word.

New language

now

Review language

Road safety instructions

Bring to the lesson

- the Tape
- the Flashcards for car, bus, van and bike
- the Flashcards for Karim, Samir and Leila.
- (Optional) string/rope
- speech bubbles for *We can go.* and *We can't go.*

Preparation

- (Optional) Bring in some rope, string or other marker for Warm-up and Activity 2.
- Make two speech bubbles out of paper or card. One should say *We can go.* The other should say *We can't go.*

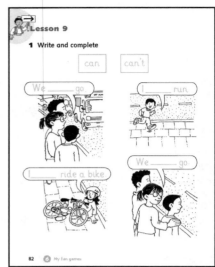

PB **page 78**   WB **page 82**

Warm-up

> **Note:** If you have space in the classroom, children can act out this activity.

- Two children act the child characters and 4 children hold the vehicle Flashcards. Lay the string/rope on the floor to mark the edge of the road.

- Instruct the two children *Wait ... . Go.* They take one step forward over the line. The first child with a Flashcard then holds it up. Class says, e.g. *Be careful of the van!* The children must step back behind the line and the van 'drives' along the road.

- Continue with the other vehicles.

Presentation

- Play the *Traffic game* on the board to practise *Be careful of ... .* Use the Flashcards for Karim, Samir and Leila for crossing the road.

- Set up the Karim, Samir and Leila Flashcards on the board with lines in front of them to mark the road. Explain that they are waiting to cross the road.

- Put the car Flashcard on the road going towards the characters. Ask the class *Can you see a car?* Class answers *Yes.*

- Stick the speech bubble *We can't go.* beside the characters. Say the words.

- 'Drive' the car along the road.

- Go through the same process with the bus.

- The third time, ask *Can you see a car/bus?* Class answers *No.*

- Put the speech bubble *We can go.* beside the characters. Say the words and move the figures across the 'road'.

page 78

🎧 1 Listen and read

- Children look at the pictures for a few moments. Ask them what is happening.

- Tell them to listen and follow the words in their books. Play the Tape.

Tapescript

Narrator: Topic 6. Lesson 9. Activity 1. Listen and read.

Samir: Stop! Look left.

Look right!

Leila: Can you see the bus?

Karim: We can't go.

Toddler: I can run.

Karim: Stop! Be careful of the bus!

Leila: Be careful!

Mother: Oh! Thank you!

Samir: Now we can go!

- Explain that *Be careful* can be used as a general warning on its own. Read the speech bubbles. Class repeats. Play the Tape a second time. Children follow in their books.

- Divide the class into five groups. Each group reads a character together. Make sure children are following the story by saying the number of each picture. E.g. Say *Picture 1*. Group 1 reads *Stop! Look left! Look right!* Say *Picture 2*. Group 2 reads *Can you see the bus?* and so on. Change parts and read again.

2 Act it out

- Divide children into groups of five to act out the dialogue in Activity 1. See if they can remember what the characters say without looking at the book. If they can't, let them point to each picture and read from the book.

- If there is space, let them stand at the front facing the class in a line, waiting to cross the road, like the characters in the book. The little boy can run into the road when his mother drops her shopping in the third picture.

- Alternatively, children sit at their desks and read the parts out.

- If you have some unconfident children, let them follow what the others say and then carry the bus Flashcard and 'drive' along the road.

- Let as many groups as possible act out the story.

Extension activity

- Children act out the same scene, but change the vehicle.

page 82

1 Write and complete

- Children write over the words in the boxes. They look at the scenes and write over the words in each speech bubble. They then complete the sentences by writing the correct word from the boxes in the spaces.

Lesson 10

Performance indicators

Children will be able to:
- sing a song naming each letter of the alphabet
- write initial letters of five consonant/vowel/consonant words
- fill in missing letters of the alphabet and number sequences.

New language

The words of the song

Review

The letters of the alphabet

Bring to the lesson
- the Tape
- the alphabet Flashcards

 PB **page 79**   **WB** **page 83**

Warm-up
- Play any game that your class has enjoyed.

Presentation
- Put or write all the alphabet letters on the board. Prompt the class to say the names of the letters all the way through.
- If children can say the alphabet without any help, let them say it together.

 PB **page 79**

 1 Sing
- Children look at the letters. If necessary go through them again with children saying the names of letters and pointing in their books.
- Play the Tape. Children listen and follow in their books.

Tapescript

Narrator: Topic 6. Lesson 10. Activity 1. Sing.

Child: a b c d e f g

       h i j k l m n o p

       q r s t u v w

       x y and z.

       Now I know my a, b, c,

       You can sing this song with me!

- Play the Tape again. Encourage children to join in with the song.

2 Listen, say and write
- Children look at the pictures. Point to the van, the box and the sun. Elicit the words.
- Point to the bed and pin. Name them and make sure children understand what they are.
- Play the Tape. Children repeat in the first pause. In the second they repeat and write the letter which begins the word.

Tapescript

Narrator: Topic 6. Lesson 10. Activity 2. Listen, say and write.

Adult: Van. [pause] Van. [pause]

Bed. [pause] Bed. [pause]

Pin. [pause] Pin. [pause]

Box. [pause] Box. [pause]

Sun. [pause] Sun. [pause]

- Point again to the pictures in the book. Prompt the words.
- Write *van* on the board. Point to the first letter and elicit /v/. Then prompt the whole word. Do the same with the other words.

Extension activity

- Give out all the alphabet Flashcards. Children sing the song and stand up with their Flashcard when their letter is mentioned. Make sure every child gets the chance to do this.

 page 83

1 Find and write

- Children read through the alphabet and write in the missing letters. Point out that the complete alphabet is given to help them.

2 Find and write

- Children look at the sequence of numbers and fill in those that are missing.

Lesson 11 – Review

Performance indicators

Children will be able to:
- use and understand the language taught in Lessons 1–10

Review language

The language from Topics 1–6

Bring to the lesson

- all reading word cards from Topics 4–6
- a list of 10 instructions

Preparation

Write a list of 10 questions and instructions (see Extension activity).

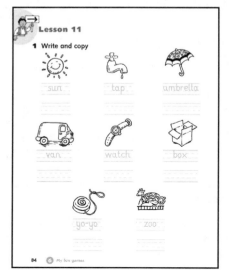

 page 80

 page 84

Warm-up

- Use word cards to practise all the reading words the children have learned in Topics 4 to 6.

Presentation

- Practise some of the instructions that will be part of the game. Ask randomly around the class, e.g. *What is it? What begins with … ? Name a toy/colour/animal.*

- Explain the phrase *kind of transport* then ask a child to name one.

 page 80

1 Play the game

- Children choose a balloon. Give them a task according to the number they choose. See the list of questions and instructions below.

- This can be played with the whole class, repeating some tasks to give every child a turn.

- Alternatively, divide the class into small groups. Children answer your questions and follow your instructions together. They do the actions together, count together or help each other to think of items.

Teacher questions and instructions

1 What is it?

2 What begins with b? Name 2.

3 Name three kinds of transport.

4 Name four toys.

5 Hop five times.

6 Clap your hands six times.

7 Name seven animals.

8 Jump eight times.

9 Name nine colours.

10 Count to 10.

Extension activity

- In teams play a game like the one in the Pupil's Book, alternating questions and instructions between two or more teams.

- Make up your own list of questions and instructions, asking anything that you think your class should be able to do, and using any objects or Flashcards that you choose. Questions might be, e.g. *What is it? What colour is it? How many … ?* You could include instructions such as, e.g. *Stand up, look left,* etc.

- If one team cannot answer or does the wrong action the other team can try.

 page 84

1 Write

- Children write over the alphabet exemplar words in the grid below each picture. They then copy the words into the grids below. Go around checking that they are forming letters correctly.

- To extend this activity, ask the children to colour each picture using one or two colours. These can be used in a variety of ways:

1 Whole class activity

- Ask children *What can you see?* A child points in his/her book and answers, e.g. *I can see a blue and white umbrella.*

- Ask *What colour is the van/box/watch?* etc. Children answer according to the colours they have used.

2 Pairs/groups activity

- Children ask each other questions like those above.

- They can also put their books on the table and talk about all the pictures, e.g. *I can see two red vans.*

3 Team game

- A child from Team A must ask a correct question for a point and Team B answers for one point. Then they change over.

Lesson 12

Performance indicators

Children will be able to:
- use and understand the language taught in *Caravan 1*.

Review language

actions
I can/can't ...

Bring to the lesson

- the Tape
- the Flashcards for actions
- the word cards for actions
- the alphabet Flashcards
- a selection of other Flashcards and word cards (see Extension activity)

PB **page 81**   WB **page 85**

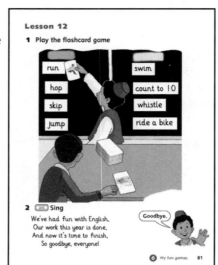

Warm-up

- Children sing their favourite song from any of the topics.
- Children play their favourite game from any of the topics.

Presentation

- Hold up each of the action Flashcards in turn. Invite children to say the word.
- Hold up the Flashcards in a different order. Invite children to say *I can ...* and do the action (they mime *swim* and *ride a bike*).
- Hold up the word cards in a different order. Children read.

 PB **page 81**

1 Play the Flashcard game

- Put the word cards for actions on the board as shown in the book, any four on each side.
- Put the matching Flashcards face down in a pile on your desk.

- The class plays in two teams, taking turns to pick up a Flashcard from the pile. If it matches a word on their side they put the Flashcard beside the correct word. If it doesn't match, or if they put it in the wrong place, the Flashcard must be put back at the bottom of the pile.
- When a child has correctly matched a Flashcard, e.g. jump, he/she chooses someone from his/her team to come forward. This child must say, e.g. *I can jump* to win another point.
- The whole team repeats and does the action for a third point.

 **2 Sing**

- Say the words of the song to the class, waving on *goodbye*.
- Explain to the class that the song is about the end of lessons in school.
- Play the Tape. Children listen.

Tapescript

Narrator: Topic 6. Lesson 12. Activity 2. Sing.

Children: We've had fun with English,

But our work this year is done,

And now it's time to finish,

So goodbye, everyone!

- Play it a second time and encourage them to join in with the words and to wave on the last line.

- Teach the song by writing it on the board. Say each line. Children repeat.

- Rub out one or two significant words in each line. Children say the line filling in the words.

- Continue until all the words are rubbed off and children say the whole verse without prompts.

- They can then sing the song themselves, accompanied just by the music.

Extension activity

- Play the Flashcard game from Activity 1 with a different set of Flashcards and word cards, e.g. animals, toys, transport, or mix them up. Children match pictures to words.

- Use the small sets of alphabet exemplars and word cards so that children can do this activity in small groups, matching pictures and words.

 page 85

- If you wish, you may use this page as a test to check on class progress in work covered in Topic 6. Give children a fixed length of time to complete each activity. Make sure the children know what to do before they start.

- Alternatively, you can use this page as normal Workbook activities and explain each task in turn, keeping the whole class working together.

1 Write

- Children write over the words in the bubbles then write the correct action word to complete the sentence. You may wish to leave the appropriate word cards on the board for children to check spelling.

2 Write *Stop* or *Go*

- Children look at the pictures and colour the lights red or green. They write the words in the correct spaces.

3 Write *Yes I can* or *No I can't*

- Children look at the pictures and write the appropriate answer in the small bubbles.

Resources

Introduction

The following pages can be photocopied to produce resources for use during lessons. There are 26 exemplar picture cards, each showing the artwork that appears in the *Caravan* Pupil's Book and Workbook: there are a further four picture cards for the main classroom items; and there are templates for producing cut-out socks and birds for use in Topic 3, Lessons 10 and 12. The Preparation sections in the teaching notes tell you what resources you need in which lessons, and how many of each you need to make.

Preparation instructions

When you know how many of each resource you need, the procedures for making them are as follows.

> **You will need:**
> Cardboard or stiff paper
> Glue
> Scissors

Picture cards

● Photocopy as many of the required pages as you need.
● Stick the pages on to pieces of card to make them last longer.
● Cut around each individual card.
● Store the cards in an envelope or box until needed. Store the cards between lessons, as you can use them again.

Sock and bird templates

● Photocopy as many of the required page as you need.
● Cut out each template.
● Store the templates in an envelope or box until needed. The children will colour these resources in, so they can be reused for practising colour vocabulary.

Further resources

There are other resources used in *Caravan* that will need to be made specially. Again, instructions are given in the teaching notes about what resources are needed when. The resources are as follows:

● Letter cards (lower and upper case)
● Number cards
● Dotted number cards (large and small)
● Colour cards
● Word cards
● Optional picture cards

Preparation

Letter cards

Cut out 26 cards. If possible, make these the same size as those on pages 163–167 (4.5cm x 7cm). Use a black marker to write one letter (lower or upper case) of the alphabet on each card.

Number cards

Cut out 10 cards. If possible, make these the same size as those on pages 163–167 (4.5cm x 7cm). Use a black marker to write one number from 1–10 on each card.

Dotted number cards (large and small)

Cut out 2 sets of 10 cards. If possible, one set should be the same size as those on pages 163–167 (4.5cm x 7cm). The other set should be about A4 size. Each card in the sets should have a pattern of dots on it, from 1 up to 10 (see page 17 of the Pupil's Book).

Colour cards

To make a colour card, cut out a piece of card. If possible, it should be the same size as those on pages 163–167 (4.5cm x 7cm). Use coloured markers to colour the card in, or glue on pieces of coloured paper, etc.

Word cards

To make a word card, cut out a piece of card. A good size is 14cm by 5cm. Use a black marker to write on the words you need. (See teaching notes for details.)

Optional picture cards

For the games mentioned in the teaching notes you may wish to produce picture cards for items of vocabulary other than the four main classroom items. To do this follow the procedure for producing the Letter or Number cards. For pictures you can either draw the items yourself, following the artwork in the Pupil's Book, or cut out and photocopy pictures from magazines, etc.

Picture Cards

Alphabet exemplars: a–f

© Macmillan Publishers Limited 2004. This sheet may be photocopied and used within the classroom.

Picture Cards

Alphabet exemplars: g–l

© Macmillan Publishers Limited 2004. This sheet may be photocopied and used within the classroom.

PHOTOCO

Picture Cards

Alphabet exemplars: m–r

© Macmillan Publishers Limited 2004. This sheet may be photocopied and used within the classroom.

Picture Cards

Alphabet exemplars: s–x

© Macmillan Publishers Limited 2004. This sheet may be photocopied and used within the classroom.

Picture Cards

**Alphabet
exemplars: y–z**

**Classroom
objects**

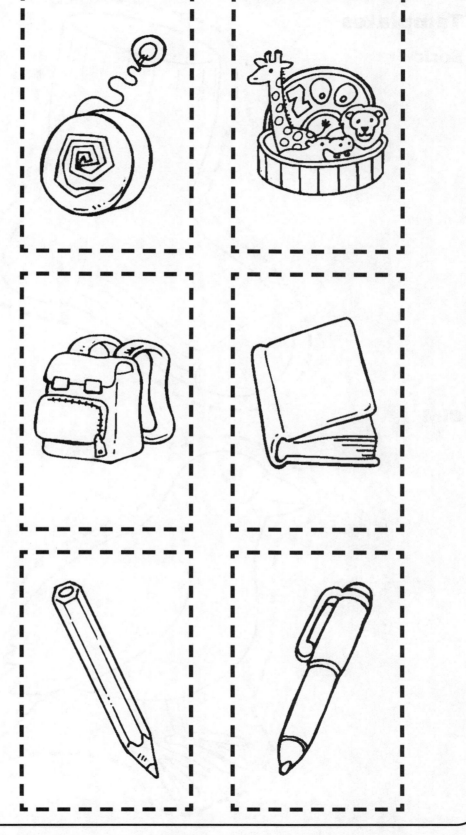

© Macmillan Publishers Limited 2004. This sheet may be photocopied and used within the classroom.

PHOTOCOPIABLE

Templates

Sock

Bird

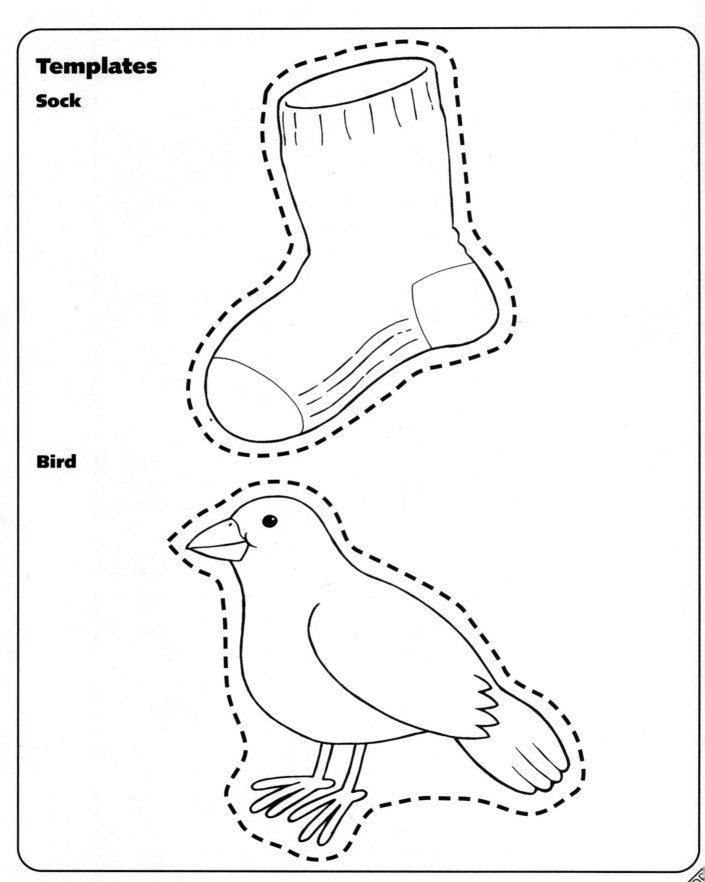

© Macmillan Publishers Limited 2004. This sheet may be photocopied and used within the classroom.